CHRIST ON PARNASSUS

BY THE SAME AUTHOR

CONGREGATIONALISM AND REUNION 5s. net
FAITH, FREEDOM, AND THE FUTURE 15s. net
GOD THE HOLY FATHER 9s. 6d. net
POSITIVE PREACHING AND THE MODERN MIND 12s. 6d. net
THE CHURCH AND THE SACRAMENTS 15s. net
THE CRUCIALITY OF THE CROSS 8s. 6d. net
THE JUSTIFICATION OF GOD 10s. 6d. net
THIS LIFE AND THE NEXT 7s. 6d. net
THE PERSON AND PLACE OF JESUS CHRIST 15s. net
THE PRINCIPLE OF AUTHORITY 21s. net
THE SOUL OF PRAYER 7s. 6d. net
THE WORK OF CHRIST 15s. net

INDEPENDENT PRESS LTD

CHRIST ON PARNASSUS

LECTURES ON ART,
ETHIC, AND THEOLOGY

BY

PETER TAYLOR FORSYTH

M.A., D.D.

Eugene ♦ Pasadena
1996

Christ on Parnassus
by P. T. Forsyth

First Published 1911 by
Hodder and Stoughton Ltd.

ISBN: 1-57910-014-7

Printed By  1996
790 East 11th Avenue • Eugene, OR 97401

TO THE

ELECT LADY

WHOM I LOVE IN TRUTH,

AND NOT I ONLY,

BUT ALSO ALL WHO KNOW HER

PREFACE

THESE lectures were an attempt to commend to an audience more or less popular but cultivated the principle that religion, and especially Christianity, if real and deep, affects the whole man and the whole society. For that purpose I took a great social product that often seems to have less to do with Christianity than some others—namely Art. And with this main object in view I made the further attempt to introduce to notice the work in this kind of, perhaps, the greatest and richest mind that ever gave itself to such a question. The *Æsthetik* of Hegel is, perhaps, the finest of all his works. And if taken with, say, Lessing's *Laocöon*, it would form a liberal education in *litterae humaniores*, and provide such a basis of equipment for the spiritual critic as but too seldom exists. I will confess that I was less concerned that everything I said should escape challenge than that those who heard should get some idea of a great method in these matters, and realise how high, subtle, and manifold the paths of the Spirit are on the way to its evolution as Holy Spirit. In the first part of the book, therefore, I am preaching Hegel, not, I hope, without judgment, but certainly as the text I expound. In the latter part I am less dependent on him, and, I fear, worth less. But I am not without evidence that the lectures to some opened new vistas, and to some few a new world. And I am hopeful that some suggestive virtue may not quite leave them when they go into print. They mean nothing for a philosophy of æsthetic, beyond what Hegel did. But I should be glad to think that they helped any to believe, first, that a Gospel which saves society must also save its culture; and, second, that a great philosophy has a fine and powerful word to say on other things than metaphysic,—on things that express the passion, romance, and beauty of life. A scientific treatment of history (if we get the right science) will do justice also to the imagination in which the spiritual powers blossom for a life beyond life.

PREFACE

Much attention is now happily given to the philosophy both of history and religion, and it may be worth while to urge that no account of society is just which ignores the action, in it and for it, of the spiritual power which comes next to religion, and has so many exchanges with it. In an age of culture the artist in various kinds means much. And, lest anything so fatal should take place as the substitution of an æsthetic for an ethical religion, or art be depraved by being idolised, it is well that we should know what art cannot do through those who duly own what it can. The glacial age is now over when religion was in peril from natural science; in our more genial day the danger is from other and sunnier sides; and one of these is the æsthetic. Truly the danger of Capua to Hannibal is great. But it may be useful, while some show how bad a master Art may be, that others should indicate how good she can be as a servant. If a bad judge she is a precious witness. That is what I try to suggest to any aspiring and ingenuous spirits who may happen to take this book into their hands. Considerations of the kind become more valuable as we need more and more to supplement the ruling social interests with a public concern that leans to the spiritual rather than the economic side. The National Gallery represents an interest as integral to the Church in its own way as the national Parliament.

* * * * *

I am very grateful to my colleague, Dr. Bennett, for his vigilance and suggestions on the proofs.

CONTENTS

I

GREEK ART AND RELIGION 1

II

GREEK ART AND RELIGION—*Continued* . . . 22

III

HEBREW ART AND RELIGION 43

IV

CHRISTIAN ART IN ITS GENERAL FEATURES . . 75

V

PAINTING—I 98

VI

CHRISTIANITY AND PAINTING—II 128

VII

ARCHITECTURE, ESPECIALLY CHRISTIAN . . . 160

VIII

MUSIC 192

IX

POETRY 226

X

ART, ETHIC, AND RELIGION 255

I
GREEK ART AND RELIGION

I PROPOSE in these lectures to trace some of the relations that exist between two subjects each of absorbing interest, and one at least of an importance quite transcendent. Art and Religion have always been closely connected, and they have exerted on each other an influence which not only gives scope for much variety of opinion, but opens regions of inviting speculation on some of the rarest qualities and energies of the human spirit.

Experience shows it to be a foolish, and even mischievous, effort to pronounce perpetual divorce between Art and Religion. Quarrel they may and they do, but it is not alienation; and it is not for a third party to interfere, or a jury of either artists, apostles, or critics to decree more than a judicial, and perhaps temporary, separation. The spirit of Religion *will*, in certain phases, strive towards an utterance of itself in the forms of art; the forms of art will again and again become the vehicle, or even the source, of certain phases of religion; and the inner spirit of art moves among realms and powers which for many do the work of religion on their souls (however their conscience may fare). The inward grace is not lifted out of all connection with the outward, nor has the outward as yet lost its strange power to stir and kindle the inward. But we know how hard and delicate a problem it is to adjust in our own lives the conflicting claims of soul and sense. And it is a problem of much greater delicacy and difficulty to reconcile the spirit with its artistic expression—whether our aspiration be perfectly to utter soul by form, or only to give the soul such utterance as shall be a point of rest for it, without becoming a seduction to tarry or waver on its upward flight.

It may be found in such an inquiry that we reach a result like this. We could not, in view of the facts, say that the influence of Religion upon Art had been mischievous, seeing that it is Religion which, for the most part, has called Art into existence, and supplied it with its very finest and loftiest inspirations. Nor could we go so far as to say that the influence of Art on Religion had been deleterious on the whole. In many respects it has been, but it could not be maintained that the balance has been on the mischievous side. But this at least may safely be said, in the first place, that, with the one exception of Greece (to be afterwards referred to), the influence of Religion upon Art has been more powerful than the influence of Art on Religion; and, in the second place, that it has been more beneficial. Religion has done more for Art than Art has done, or is likely to do, for

Religion. And this is true, whether you take the word influence in a quantitative or a qualitative sense, whether you regard its amount or its kind.

And this is only what we should expect from the nature of the case. Religion is a controlling, guiding power in life, but Art is not. Even Goethe said, Art is a comrade and not a guide. Religion lies nearer the conscience and its demand. It is a master in a sense in which Art is not. Art is but a stately servant of the highest life—a servant to be trusted, even to be loved, to be held always in great honour and state ; but a servant still and no lord, not the fountain of dignity, nor the final appeal, not admitted to the most private hours or holy scenes, not allowed to be conversant with everything its lord doeth or intimate with his final purpose. Religion handles realities, creates an obligation, and assures a destiny which Art does but try to represent. There are hours of contact with reality which are so sacred and solemn that we react from the idea of their being represented, or even published, in any way. There are spiritual things so spiritually discerned that it is irreverence to attempt to body them sensibly forth. They are things not lawful for a man to utter. When God was painted so that He could be hung by posterity over a doorway in the South Kensington Museum, an audacity had rushed into Art which was the sure index and presage of its decline ; and a kind of apology was furnished for employing it in the baser service of man. Art in its very hour of perfection had become irreverent ; and irreverence in Art is as repulsive, as significant and premonitory of moral decay, as a sneer in a woman however handsome or smart. Art, then, is but the servant and representative, though not the vassal, of Faith, to be surrounded with all the state and honour due to the ambassador of a mighty king, but no more to be placed in supreme control of life than an angel is to be put in supreme charge of home or State.

With this as the fundamental relationship between them, I wish to trace broadly the progress of Art under the influence of Religion in certain phases of its existence. I will deal first with Hellenic Art and Religion, then with Hebrew Art and Religion, then with the growth and nature of Christian Art, and then with the intrinsic bearing of Christianity on Art—meaning their natural relations rather than their past history. We may take Greece as the great historic representative of Art, and ask how Art was related to Religion there. We take Israel as the grand historic representative of Religion, and ask how Religion was related to Art there. Then we take Christianity as the fusion of Jew and Gentile, and ask how the two subtlest of human energies disposed themselves in the union, and what mutual development they took.

It is a happy fortune that has made us all familiar, if it be only by casts, sketches, or photographs, with the great and perfect plastic art of Greece. I wish the same wisdom would go on to make it possible that some competent persons should speak to us on this subject, of a Sunday afternoon or evening, in a very presence of these unique productions, in the very buildings where they are stored and guarded. But it is a matter of satisfaction that so much has been done to familiarise us with the remnants and copies of ancient plastic Art. Much less has been done, however (probably much less can be done), to make the same public acquainted with the spirit of Greek Religion or the genius of Greek Imagination. I hope we may soon see the day when the unscientific mistake of pressing on the young an education mainly scientific shall have run its course, and a more cultivated and humane idea of education take its place. No doubt a real education in science is a great improvement on the gerund-grinding which used to be called classical instruction. But it is hard to believe that a knowledge of the facts of science, or even the culture of the scientific observation, can either come as natural to youth's plastic time, or be as beneficial to the community in its result, as an appeal made to that imagination which is so prompt in youth and so pliant in art. I hope, if we escape the materialistic and pedestrian habit of mind which in most people tends to be the result of an education purely scientific, we may return to a system of instruction which shall appeal to the imagination, wake up the sense of heroism and beauty, and give it an interest, other than mere curiosity, in the great achievements of the human spirit or the memorable expressions of human faith. After all, to a man or a woman, a woman or a man is more interesting, and more significant, and more lovely than even a crayfish, or a stratum, or a gem, or a tree, a moss, a flower, a cloud. And the struggle, the pathos, the tragedy, the majesty of the human spirit is both more touching and more guiding than the old convulsions of rock and sea, or the slow, cold grandeur of the passing, but pitiless heavens. Some may, perhaps, hope for a day when there shall be that in our general, and especially in our advanced, education which shall help us better than now to interpret by sympathy the intelligible forms of ancient faith, and the fair humanities of old Religion.

The average man is not always favourably impressed with the human element in old Religion. He is apt to find the human more conspicuous in it than the humane. He remembers, from his readings in classical mythology, some stories in poor taste and worse ethic. What is not impure he finds ridiculous, and the whole seems an amusing tissue of passions too like our own. He has been taught to construe his Ovid, but he has not been taught to feel Ovid's charm. He has spelled out the mythology in Homer, but he has never once caught his breath at the gleaming vision of snow-capped Olympus, with its majestic tenantry in their solemn nooks. He did not see Apollo descend from his chariot, but only a well-built nobleman getting out of a trap. And Zeus of the ambrosial locks in a nimbus of calm majesty, whose awful nod shook heaven, never made this stout Philistine to tremble. For was he not at best but a curly giant; and the idea of trembling at a nod is too ridiculous to men who jerk out their phonetic salute as they rush past each other habitually catching metaphorical trains. Such is the result of classical education as it has too often been. And if we turn to hope that the universal religion professed by most of us may supplement this defect, and inspire reverence, sympathy, and understanding in regard to other faiths, we may be much disappointed. So that, though the Crystal Palace and the British Museum have given us some idea of Greek statuary, we are oftener impressed with the nudity than the beauty; we have no idea of Greek imagination in other forms; and we see little more in Greek religion than a heap of stories only less debasing and absurd than the mythology of the Hindoo. Whereas the Greek mythology is itself a work of exquisite art, perennial beauty, and profound suggestion. The mythology is the first and unconscious form which was assumed by the artistic genius of a race who by their birthright were artists in all they did or dreamed.

What, then, were the special features of Greek Religion ? When we have found them we may be able to see, not only how they pass naturally into art as an expression, but how it must be so, and could not be otherwise. We may see that the forces which in other races passed into an outward action or elaborate ritual here took external shape in art. We may see that Greek Religion, by its genius, flows as naturally and inevitably into artistic production as Christianity by its genius tends to externalise itself in a Church or a philanthropy more or less elaborate and organised.

First of all, then, by its origin Greek Religion was an idealised Naturalism. The pantheon of gods was a series of personifications of natural forces and powers. Here was a link with art to begin with. If Art idealises Nature, Religion personifies it. But Nature rather than Revelation is at the basis of both. They both proceed from the action of the human spirit on visible Nature.

But though all naturalistic religions have this origin, they are not all determined into perfect Art as their flower and crown. What was it in the relation of the Greek spirit to Nature which gave it this special unique and successful bias to Art?

The development of the human mind follows the sun. Its course of empire takes its way westward. The oldest of its products are to be met with in the remote East. India is the teeming land where we find the first distinct traces of the interaction of spirit and nature. And what relation has the one to the other in that venerable Hindoo past? What is the specific oriental type of religion? What is its spiritual formation? It is the worship of the vast. It is the dominion of bigness. Spirit is in subjection to matter. It cannot throw off the load of material immensity. It is the victim of a despotism of sheer mass and force. This slavery is reflected in the political despotism which is the oriental type of government. And it is reflected also in Hindoo art. It is the art of the colossal—the art of the monstrous, whether in size or shape. The spirit is weighed upon by Nature. It is crushed by it. It does not succeed in printing its own law or features on Nature. Hence Indian art is mainly, if not entirely, imitative art. It is not inventive, not creative, not commanding. It utters no soul. It is the activity of lawless imagination, which has no ideal in itself, but riots in reflecting or decorating the crushing exuberance of that vast and prolific land. Hence you have the cave temples of Elephanta, more impressive than grand, with their huge and often hideous images. You have the profuse and barbaric use of colours and gems so conspicuous everywhere.

Pass westward. Come to Egypt. Here, amid many features which remind you of India, you have also something more. You have the spirit still staggering under the vastness of Nature and its inexorability. You have the Pyramids, colossal tombs. You have interminable catacombs stored with mummies. You have temples little less vast than the great shrines of the Indian peninsula. You have the Sun and the Nile as the dominant powers. But you have also something more. In the Pyramids you have the most intricate exactitude of measurements. On the face of the fields you have the slate on which were worked the first theorems of geometry. In the mummies you have a dry and harsh, but powerful utterance of faith in the defiance of death and the Immortality of the Soul. You have a Book of the Dead. You have, that is, the laws of the reason, and the separateness and persistence of the spirit, asserted over against the vastitude of Nature. You no more find the spirit quite passive and crushed beneath its external volume. You find the struggle for emancipation begun. The inert stone is more than a mere copy of the world without. It begins to be a reflection of the world within. You have the worship of animals in full course, the worship of *life*, which is a step at least from the worship of the material world. You have the hieroglyphics. And what are these but natural objects which, instead of weighing down the mind, are made symbols harnessed by the mind to its purpose, and taught to draw a load of rational meaning. You have in fine the powers of Nature, personified and worshipped indeed, but transformed at the same time, tinged with the colour of the human spirit, and not copied merely, but shaped. Mind is not the slave of Nature, but now appears as in struggle with Nature, up on one knee, as it were, and insisting on a force and nature of its own. And the crowning expression of this is to be found in the specific Egyptian symbol, the Sphinx, which is half beast half woman, half Nature half Spirit, half mastery, half mystery.

Now return to Greece. We are no more in a barbaric world, though we are in the world of naturalism still. We have no more of that worship of the vast, nor even of that colossal struggle to escape from it, or at least to vindicate for the soul a place over against it; but we have the worship of Nature still. It is Nature, however, with an addition and a difference. A huge step has been taken? What is added? Man has been added as part, but the capital part, of Nature. It might be said that man was part of Nature in the Hindoo

GREEK ART AND RELIGION

faith. Yes, but he was a crushed part of it. He was the tortoise which was under the elephant which was under the earth. But here he is on an equality with Nature. And he is not only on an equality with it, but in harmony with it. Independence makes the real concord. Freedom makes the true unity. There is a fine play and balanced action between them: and that results in beauty.

The tendency of Greek thought was pantheistic. So is also the tendency of Hindoo thought. But this grand difference has been pointed out. India houses the Pantheon of the Imagination, Greece the Pantheon of Thought. In India Imagination ran riot upon the boundless and ever-changing lines of Nature. In Greece man found his own eternal laws imprinted, reflected in Nature, and by a pre-established harmony she became his friend, his ally, his equal, his consort. I am anxious not to use expressions which would indicate that at last Nature had become the faithful servant and trusty organ of the human spirit, to be taken up or laid down by that spirit on its free occasions or spontaneous impulses; because that was a step yet to be taken—taken by Christianity. It is there that we find the soul really above Nature, and charged with a revelation which Nature could never adequately express. And therefore I say guardedly that in Greece the Humanity had struggled from beneath the heel of Nature to a footing of equality, friendship, and harmony with it. The soul had not yet become conscious of wants, and secrets, and powers which were beyond the reach of matter to express.

As yet the two dwelt together in naive equality, and Nature was as yet a perfect, or not inadequate, vehicle for the soul at the stage of development to which it had come.

It would be wrong to say that Greek religion was not reverent, but its reverence was a small part of it compared with other faiths, such as the Hebrew. And the reason is clear. Man found all Nature, indeed all existence, culminating in himself. His gods were but magnified, and very natural, men. They, like himself, were under the great dark Fate. It was not the gods that made man, it was man that made the gods. They were the projections of himself in his moods, passions, thoughts, and imaginations. The Greek began by personifying Nature; true, but he ended by apotheosising himself, his high natural self. He took the power of Nature, vivified it with his own mind, clothed it in his own emotion, and adorned it with his own personal beauty. They were splendid creatures, those Olympians—but creatures. There was no gulf unspeakable between them and their subjects. They mixed with men in wonderful freedom. They exchanged passion as well as thought. The gods were not moral governors. Their worshippers might bow, but were not abased before them. Holiness had a meaning in Greece quite different from what it had in Israel. It was the immune and not the pure. Sin was hardly known or understood. Awe there was before these divinities, but it was not breathless and speechless; it was hardly reverence. It could still express itself without fire-purged lips.

It never lost a feeling of parity between men and gods which reflected the perfect understanding between man and Nature. It was a happy creed. The Greek dreaded some aspects of Nature intensely; but he had the lucky power of casting them out of his thought; and when he looked Nature in the face again, he found it easy to forget that she had ever been cruel, or even coy. In Greece we have the world's youth, now for ever gone under the pressure of vaster interests, higher powers, and severer cares. We have there the gay adolescence of a mind and body perfectly balanced and sane, the sunny gladness of a time and a clime where Nature and man met each other half-way, and matter and spirit kissed without stooping. This religion was the apotheosis of natural joy. What wonder that its worshippers became artists in spite of themselves, and, without knowing it, touched a completeness of perfection which the world, now larger, sees no more, nor ever again perhaps shall see.

And then it was all so genial and easy, this creed. It was a creed of immanence, not of urgency. The Divine filled them, but it laid no heavy burdens on the shoulders of its votaries. It bade them be themselves and they would do well as organs of immanent divinity. It did not control them, but at the same time it did not stunt them. It did not sober and steady them, true; but also it did not pinch and distort them. It was a pure and free naturalism, culminating in man himself. This creed had no founder whose specific personality should define and steady the course of its after-development, but a reverence for whom might also impoverish the types of character in the worshippers, and their modes of faculty. It had no priestly caste to sit with deadly obscurantism upon all new growth, to spread through the moral air its peculiar contagion, and emit the miasma so fatal to adventurous spiritual endeavour. And it had no sacred Koran hung round the neck of living men, with a weight of final dogma, and the cast-iron exemplar of a single type of thought and life. Never was the soul of the natural man so free, so favoured, for the realising of all that it is within the scope of the natural man to do. The Greek soul moved as freely, and therefore as gracefully, under the impulse of its religion as the Greek body beneath the crystalline ether where it so joyfully paced. It is a conspicuous sign of this religion that, pagan though it be, there is in it little or no superstition. Fear was cast out by the perfect love of beauty, grace, and joy. Their religion was as healthy as their life and thought. It has been called the Religion of Beauty. It might just as well be called the Religion of Joy. The bright shining heaven which their old Indian and European forefathers first worshipped as God was never so clearly glassed, so purely and powerfully reflected, as in the mirror of the Hellenic consciousness.

Such was the character of Greek Religion. How was it, now, that it tended inevitably to take form in a perfect Art, and make its artists its prophets, and its prophets artists (like Æschylus)? What the prophet was to the Jew, that was the artist to the Greek. It was the artist more than any other man that deepened and refined the Greek consciousness of the divine. Greece is, perhaps, the only land of which it can be said that its artists gave to their religion more than they received. This is possible only with a type of religion whose inevitable goal and consummation was Art. How was it, then, that this Religion was bound to have this goal and inevitably pass into Art; to have Art for its most congenial ritual, and works of Art for the works of its law? In other creeds Art is, and can be, but the handmaid and adjutant of piety. It is the delicate blossom and graceful foliage of faith. The faith is not absorbed into the Art. It outlives the Art; and the tree sometimes sees many crops, many styles and schools of Art, rise and die. Here, on the contrary, Art is the faith's fruit, which in turn becomes its seed. It is the perfect development of Religion; and not only so, its works become the germs or centres round which a minor religious feeling gathered in the later centuries, when the mythology was believed no more, and the philosophies had become very dry. Like Lear in the arms of Cordelia, the old Greek religion died in the embrace of its beautiful daughter Art. It was but in its youth that the nation was naïvely religious. In its maturity its religion became æsthetic. And it spent its old age, without any faith, among monuments which were texts more than aspirations, in the sad and feeble contemplation of the artistic glories of its manliest and, in the Greek sense, godliest years. If the Apollo Belvedere may be taken as the symbol of the people's youth, the calm majestic dignity of the Sophocles in the Vatican may be allowed to stand for its maturity; and then we may figure its later years as the pathetic return upon his past of the old Œdipus, blind and shattered, led by the hand of the noble daughter whose beauty he could not see, but whose inner nobility he could feel, and whose presence was a help and a stay, a dim reality and a dear memory of the bright, the beautiful, and the brave.

To explain this irresistible determination of Greek religion to Art, it is not enough to fall back simply on the free and copious joy of the Greek in the presence of Nature. That itself may require explanation. And in other races we do not find that their measure of natural joy finds an artistic expression in any form of art as full as the joy. There is nothing in Scandinavian art, with its note of the melancholy North, to express to us the, doubtless, intense joy which Dane and Norseman had in taming the sea (which the Greeks so feared), and conquering provinces out of its shore. There must be something else which gave the Greek the power to utter his joy in Nature as no other race has done. Art means more than the overflow of natural joy and the cry of delight in Nature's beauty. Perfect art is something more than the musical vibration of a susceptible soul when struck by the finger of Nature. It is not tumultuous, it is bridled emotion. It is passion working under law, fervent, but not ungovernable, working,

GREEK ART AND RELIGION 17

too, under a law which really adds to its depth and its power. Art, we may at once say, is natural passion working and speaking under the free but stern control of law, thought, or spiritual form. In great Art Nature is not only answered by a full and free emotion, but it is transfused with intellect in a perfectly balanced way. Mind and matter meet and mix in perfect harmony, symmetry, and balance. If there be an excess of the natural, the material, over the spiritual or mental element, Art is gross or monstrous as in India. If there be an excess of the mental or spiritual, Art becomes inadequate. The material is tongue-tied, so to speak. It is unpleasantly, and therefore inartistically, strained and warped in the excessive effort to express more than lies in its possible sphere. Such is the case often in Christian Art. But where the spiritual compass is not too vast for the material, where the gamut of the soul, so to say, faces in Nature a keyboard of the exact length for it, then we have expression adequate to spirit and spirit satisfied with expression, we have spirit and matter in perfect accord. We have, in fact, that relation of spirit to matter which I have already indicated as the specific quality of the Greek genius, and which shaped the Greek religion; as the Greek philosophers adjusted the universe to mind without feeling an irreconcilable schism between its two manifestations in Nature and Man. Spirit and matter in complete balance, mutual service, and total harmony, in 'noble simplicity and calm magnanimity,' as Winckelmann defined it—that was the feature of Greece; and these are the conditions of perfect Art of the plastic type. The material vehicle is then completely equal to the task of expressing the spiritual content. The spiritual motive does not exceed or strain the going power of the material machine. The whole is expressed in the proverbial Greek ideal—a sound mind in a sound body. That is the fundamental canon of Greek Art, indeed you may say its charter. It was inevitable, then, that such a religion, a spiritual conception whose 'note' was the equality and mutual adequacy of Mind and Nature, Soul and Matter, should issue in a perfect Art. For religious emotion must express itself, and expression under these conditions is finished Art. Not necessarily the loftiest, or the most moving and precious art, but the most complete and perfect art. Once, and once only, in history did soul and sense thus meet and live on equal terms. It was in Greece. They passed there a time, which we may call short, of balanced and happy wedlock; then they had to part. It is the child of those glorious days that men would revere always in Greek Art.

I have already referred to the description of Greek religion as a pantheism of Thought. Pantheistic its tendencies certainly were. Yet it did not gravitate to a material pantheism, but to an intellectual. Spirit was not matter, but Spirit was wholly expressible through matter, matter was wholly adequate to Spirit. The manifestation of the god was all of him. The universe was the perfect embodiment of divinity. As our

GREEK ART AND RELIGION

Hellenic Gospel has it, the Word, the expression, was God, was completely adequate to the Spirit. What an historic person was to a holy God, that Nature, or the natural man, was to mind in Greek Art. So the resources of stone formed a sufficient vehicle for the soul of Phidias. And it would seem as if this not only were the very religion for a perfect Art, but the Religion which must go on to be absorbed in Art. When the spirit of man finds the material universe quite capable of uttering its best and loftiest, that is no more Religion. It is Art. It is soul and body in one accord. No more is to be said or done till the spirit receive such an accession of strength or insight as carries home the inadequacy of Nature, and casts the soul upon the resources of the Unseen and Eternal in longing, dependence, and prayer. And that is what Christianity did. Christianity said the Word expressed God adequately, but did not absorb the whole of God. The Godhead was more than the Son. God, as Father, was more than any manifestation of Him, even in a Son, could be. But the Greek God was not; he was but a superman. The Christian Incarnation was a revelation, it was not an exhaustive manifestation. How could there be such a complete manifestation of the Infinite? Yet the infinite was by Christianity forced on men as they had never felt it before. And in doing that Christianity may have given birth to a greater art, but it is a question whether it has not, at the same time, made impossible ever again a perfect art. There is a greatness far beyond æsthetic perfection. The perfect is not the absolute. The sense of the Infinite—a sense unknown to the Greeks—is not destructive of Art, but it is incompatible with an art perfect as Greece was perfect. It is incompatible with plastic art.

And this remark may further be made in passing, that, short of thorough Pantheism, a pantheistic element in religious thought is necessary for the life of true Art. God and Nature need not be regarded as interchangeable or identical, but an immanence of God in nature must be assured. And one reason of the artistic poverty of Rationalism was the great distance to which its deism removed God from the world, the hopeless schism which its thought placed between God and man, its suspicion and dislike of the mystic and sacramental function of creation.

So much, then, for the essential and philosophical connection between Greek Art and Religion. The history of their relations only illustrates the principles I have so poorly expressed.

It is clear that an Art proceeding from the spiritual condition of the Greeks must be an Art of form, not of colour. It was mind and its laws that the Greek infused into the material world, not heart and love. Its ideal was Plato's philosophic Republic, not Dante's heavenly rose. It was clearness of outline, perfectness of presentment, symmetry of form, that was his Art. His ethical ideas were affected by these features. The high character was harmonious and symmetrical rather than powerful, self-possessed rather than self-devoted, stoic rather than Christian. Measurement, his philo-

GREEK ART AND RELIGION

sophers told him, was the principle of all things, proportion was the secret of the coherent universe, numbers ruled all things; therefore his aim was the perfection of form and balance of mass and line. It was not the melting and fathomless suggestions of colour. The true Greek might lose himself in the admiring contemplation of an exquisite shell or the faultless mechanism of the heavens; he would not lose himself in the depths of the gentian's burning blue. We recall the vagueness of the Homeric colour terms. His was the art that works by expression rather than by suggestion. For have we not seen that his divinity was one that could be perfectly expressed in bodily form. Whereas a higher and holier God could but *indicate* himself in physical shape, and by revelation only *suggest*, or at most convey, the Infinite, never embody it. For the Incarnation was in a moral person rather than a physical body. Now the art of perfect expression is the art which deals with form; while the art of suggestion deals with the fluid and abysmal resources of colour. The special Greek art was sculpture, and all the arts in which Greece excelled were dominated by the sculptor's note and inspiration. They were the plastic arts, they were not the pictorial, they were the arts of proportion rather than of insight. They had nothing symbolic, nothing sacramental, and you find in them no such treatment of Nature as abounds in the poetry of Christianity, and corresponds with the prominence of landscape in Christian art.

II

GREEK ART AND RELIGION—*Continued*

EVERY department of Hellenic activity is a kind of art, and tends to structure, system, and form. There are four such departments at least.

1. The culture of the individual man was a work of structural art. A Nicomachean ethic still does more for English culture than a Christian (and produces, therefore, much friction with the Christian ideal). No other ancient or modern people, except the French and Germans, have given the same attention to education, and made of it a regular science and art, whether applied to the mind or the body. Greek mathematics and gymnastics are still a large feature of our educational art and method. The discipline did not apply to the mind alone. Health in its preservation and development was to the Greek almost as much of an art as is now its restoration. He built up with care his physical power and beauty; and the perfection of the human body was the precursor of the perfection of his sculptured art. His plastic art was the outcome of this perfect corporeal healthiness. There was no morbidity in the mind because he had studied the art of keeping disease out of the body.

GREEK ART AND RELIGION

2. The culture of thought took, with the Greeks, an exactitude and symmetry which we look in vain for elsewhere, in the ancient world at least. Their geometry is a type of that close and accurate habit of thought which began with the inquisitive and uncomfortable irony of Socrates; proceeded through the keen analysis, clear style, and limpid imagination of Plato; framed a philosophic vocabulary unique in its expressive exactitude till the Schoolmen and the Germans took philosophy in hand; and culminated in the encyclopædic system of Aristotle. This in its comprehensive symmetry became the ideal and inspiration of system-builders one thousand years after, when theology demanded to have done for it what Aristotle had done for physics and metaphysics.

3. The Greek polity was an art, and the Greek state was a vast work of structural art. Every Greek had his place in the political organism. No straggler was allowed to hang on the outside, and break the symmetry of its form. The Greek freemen were living stones in a stately fabric which not only pulsed with vitality, but was made to observe an organic law. The Greek mind, φύσει πολιτικός, shaped to an expression of itself the raw material of the natural man. It turned him from a man to a citizen, from an individual to a constituent, much as a poet would place the just word in his poem or a sculptor the muscle in his statue. And just as the complete Greek religion was matter quite transfused with spirit, as the man was body in exact balance with soul,

as philosophy was things articulated in thought, as art was stone perfectly uttering the inspiration of genius, so the Greek state was a democracy, where the individual atoms had all a recognised place and right in the political unity, but no individual was allowed an amount of self-assertion which would imperil the order and symmetry and freedom of the whole.

4. We have the department of spiritual production—of art proper, which I have already said was in its essence constructive and plastic, not pictorial. Greek art, we have seen, was determined into being plastic art by the peculiar quality of the Greek mind in relation to Nature, by the genius of Greek religion. I should like now to point out how in point of historic fact the different kinds of plastic art in Greece took their rise and their first development from religion.

(1) Architecture reached its glory in the temples, the buildings erected to cover and protect the shrine, or the statue, of the god. There were two Greek styles in chief, the Doric and the Ionic. The first was exceedingly simple and severe, simple but far from rude, simple with that severe unity of idea which is the mark of all the best Hellenic art. It is not an imitation of anything in Nature. It is the expression in stone of the essential idea which lay at the core of Greek religion. It is an utterance of the naturalistic Greek soul. The priesthood were very jealous of any interference with this divine simplicity, just as Catholic Rome was of the new Gothic. And it was only by degrees that the

GREEK ART AND RELIGION 25

Ionic spirit asserted its freedom of creative impulse, and began to add decoration, and to enlarge the size of the building. But when Ionic art became perfect, it was still under the dominance of the religious idea, on the one hand, and, on the other, of that same chaste severity and truthfulness of form which first made the simple Doric architecture what it was.

(2) It was thus the Ionic element of Greece that developed sculpture. Its purpose was to decorate the temple. It began in a small way. The sacred utensils of the building—vases, tripods, candlesticks, lamps, etc., gradually became the medium of the workman's religious imagination. On these he spent an honesty of work and a sense of beauty worthy of religion. 'This demand,' says an historian, 'ennobled the whole activity of the Greek artisan.' The next step was to do by hand what the poets like Homer and Hesiod had done in verse, to give the God a representation in human form. Like the architectural step, that was first allowed and then encouraged by the priests. Some people would offer statues or reliefs to the temple, others would wish for images of the god to carry away with them, especially if they were going abroad from his tutelary realm. Then came the third and greatest step, one closely, if less directly, connected with Religion. The great festivals of Greek unity were the periodic games, and these were not holidays simply, but holy days. They were religious observances, regulated by the priests, and part of the worship of the people. It was a memorable

epoch in Greek art when an edict of the priests allowed a statue of the victor to be set up crowned in the vestibule of the temple. The devèloped human physique then became the centre of a higher attention. In the palæstra the artists had always in their eyes the most perfect human forms, and all the strength and grace of Nature there they sublimated in stone. And in the temple, on a religious site, was placed the artist's ideal of what Nature at its best and divinest could do and be. In this lithe and powerful frame was a fit focus for artistic dreams of graceful action. No prescriptions or foreign traditions fettered the artist. Models were before him in plenty. All he had to do was freely to study, to understand, to reproduce, and idealise. It was a slight step further to raise these statues from being images of athletes to being ideals of the gods, and to pour into them a calm perfection which came from the quality of the artist's soul. Like the greatest works of lasting art, the statues of Phidias and Praxiteles, while they were kept true by a constant contact with the natural man of the stadium and the arena, were made reverent by being religious offerings and ideals. They would have been impossible but for the artist's belief that these gods were real individuals, not too far from us—as near as Olympus and its passions so like our own. They were not mere forces, not mere abstractions, but beings who were entirely expressible, and worthily expressed, in godlike human bodies. He believed that, and therefore he spoke in plastic form. It was a religious belief, a religious utterance, and a religious aim. It was not only to show his own art, or his own joy in Nature, that Phidias carved. He was national and religious as well as æsthetic. It was to help his fellow-countrymen better to realise and worship a noble, powerful, and Hellenic Zeus or Athene.

But now there is a somewhat interesting fact pressed on our notice in connection with the very human individuality of the Greek gods and their representations in sculpture. One of the great features of the Greek Pantheon is the distinct individuality and living humanity of its separate members. They were men in their passions, they were gods only in their power. Their deeds alone were superhuman. Their feelings were human, both in their beauty and in their meanness. Now, that being so, what are we to expect in their sculptured images? We are to expect, along with perfect beauty of form, much characterisation and even delicacy in graving the expression of human emotion, especially, of course, on the face. We should expect it to be impossible to carve Homer's Zeus without putting into his features traces of the activity of those affections which make him in the poet's pages so human a god. That is what we should expect, but we do not find it. Perfect as are the frames of the Greek statues, the faces do not contain expression. They embody, not individuals, but types. All idiosyncrasy is smoothed out of the features. They are very perfect, too perfect, but they lack the very thing that Homer's gods so conspicuously have—

they lack individuality and passion, and they possess a calm and a majesty which the early gods did not have. The idea has entered Greek thinking since the Homeric days; and we have in the Greek Art, both of Sophocles and Phidias, the irony (and some have even thought the sadness) with which the idea looks down from its sublime solitude upon its own partial and fleeting manifestations. Classic art tends to be ironical according as it is inspired. And that, perhaps, is why as the inspiration dies, the irony descends to the form of satire, just as the solemn irony of Christ sinks to the bitterness of the sect.

How is this to be accounted for? The answer is significant for our religious purpose. The fact indicates that a great change had come over the Greek conception of deity in the best minds between the time of Homer and Phidias. It is an illustration also of the vast influence on religion of men who did not make religion their vocation—of the thinkers and the artists. Greek thought had arisen in the interval between the Homeric and the great artistic age, and it had profoundly modified the national conception of the divine. We see the way in which thought acted on the poetic mythologies when we read the strictures on Homer contained in the second book of Plato's *Republic*. Homer is there censured for representing the gods as doing or causing things mean, passionate, and unworthy of a divine ideal. Now the same tendencies as produced those words of Plato were also acting before Plato upon Phidias. That

GREEK ART AND RELIGION

great artist was inspired with an ideal. He was not inspired with human sympathy, which is a Christian type of inspiration. He was inspired with an ideal which withdrew him from sympathy with the individual, characteristic, and passionate side of men, and fixed his gaze upon the calm, the majestic, the changeless, in humanity. And the work of Phidias is an illustration of a statement which I have already ventured, that in Greece, and in Greece alone, the artist gave more to traditional religion than he received from it, and did more for its purification than it did for his. It is also an illustration of another statement that the artist in Greece corresponds to the prophet in Israel. It was the function of both to reform, purify, and exalt the conceptions of God which had come down to them, and which they had, while purifying, to enforce. No one man in Greek history probably (unless it were Æschylus) did more to exalt and ennoble the popular conception of the King of the gods than Phidias by his Olympian Zeus. His work in this respect may be compared with what was done for the conception of Jehovah by Isaiah. 'This artist,' says Curtius, ' deserves the high name of a theologian. For his works were at once revelations of the divine and reflections of the soul of his race.'

So now, when we speak of the Greeks as masters of the art of expression and form, we must limit the use of the word ' expression.' As we usually understand the word, it is only under Christian influences that expression has become a power or an aim in Art. The Greeks expressed (as in the Elgin Marbles) all that the human *body* could express of perfect beauty of form, and power, and movement of Life. It was Life they uttered, however calm. But above Life is passion, and beyond passion is eternal Love. And these higher powers utter themselves in infinite variety in the human face. But the face was in the Greek statue a blank in respect of these things. It was a beautiful type. There was no portraiture. Watts had much of Phidias in him, but he could also do in portrait what Phidias could not. The Greek statue was the abstraction and idealisation of a common element found partially in most Greek faces, but entirely in none. This is illustrated also in the drama. We have the same great difference between Greek art and Christian art indicated in the fact that the actors on the Greek stage not only wore masks which made facial expression impossible, but had inserted in the masks an apparatus for magnifying the voice, which at the same time, of course, falsified it, and made it incapable of the fine inflections and shades of characteristic on which now so much depends. The theatres there as functions of the community were so vast that few only of the spectators could see the face, and without the acoustic assistance placed in the mask, but few would have heard the voice. Facial expression and phonetic inflection were therefore lost on the Greek stage. Large audiences do tend to destroy *nuances* of expression, partly because the voice must be raised above the conversational style.

And even our modern singers and speakers find that where there is an extreme exuberance of admiration in the vast popular audience, there is an inability to seize the finer beauties of their art or theme.

It is Christianity which has given to the individual that infinite value which we now feel is his; and in so doing it has opened an entirely new and infinite field to Art, the field of expression and characteristic in passion, sentiment, and affection. There is a variety and a profundity in Christian Humanity which Greek Humanism never reached. Christianity has also given us such a revelation of God that it is impossible for any artist to do for it what was done for Greek religion by Phidias. The artist can but reflect, he cannot reveal in this region; he can but suggest, and not portray; and perhaps he will find his account in abstaining altogether from spending his art on the holiest sanctities of Christian faith, where symbolism is more in place. The Eternal dwelleth not in temples made with hands.

We may also mark in passing how the tendency of Greek humanism was at last to dehumanise God, to remove Him from the sight, sense, or sympathy of human passion and pain, to set Him in an inhuman calm, either Epicurean or Stoic in its kind; whereas in Israel the tendency was just the contrary. It was to purify the divine idea, but it was to do so while humanising God.[1]

---

[1] I say this while remembering the tendency in Judaism to interpose a hierarchy of angels between God and Man. But that was borrowed from the farther East. It is quite oriental and pagan.

Instead of moving Him out of the reach of human woe, it brought Him into closer and closer sympathy with it. Instead of setting God outside life, and calmly above it, it poured Him, as it were, into life, loaded Him with its mystery, its sadness, its pity, even its horror, and charged Him with the burden of its release. The ideal servant of God was not the calm assessor of great calm Zeus, but such an one as we see in Is. liii.—formless, uncomely, rejected, bruised, chastised, and finally slain, but mighty to redeem.

(3) The third kind of art, properly so called, which the Greeks brought to a high success was poetry. This, of course, is not one of the plastic arts, but the more we study Greek poetry, the more we find the presence of that influence which made Greek art of all kinds plastic in its nature. We find in the structure of the poetry a minute attention to form, proportion, balance; and spread over the best kinds of it we find that calm, fair, and exalted harmony which is the soul of sculpture. I have already quoted one of the greatest authorities on Greek art as saying that its leading characters are 'noble simplicity and calm magnanimity.' Now that exactly describes, not only a Greek statue, but a Greek play. The acme of Greek poetic art was reached by Sophocles, and these words just express the impression left by the Antigone or the Œdipus. There is not the richness, the unfathomable sadness, and the soft, deep tenderness, the ample humour, the profound pity for the profound riddle of human destiny which we feel

GREEK ART AND RELIGION

in Shakespeare (I leave the vexed question of Euripides); but there is about these plays what I have named—the noble, statuesque calm, the magnanimous simplicity, which Phidias loved and breathed. What I have just said refers to their spirit. It is the calm which crowns the complete harmony of life and environment, or the entire ability of the poet to body forth his view of life. If one spoke of the form of the Greek drama, it would still be more easy to illustrate, in the rigid and balanced structure of both the lines, the choruses, and the acts—especially the choruses—this care bestowed on form, this exquisite chasing of the thought, bridling, and yet supporting it at every turn by the control of a sleepless law. But it would be out of place to say anything here about the structure of Greek verse.

But now, when I come to say something on the religious aspect of this art of poetry, I may and must introduce Homer. If Homer be hardly an artist in the same sense as Sophocles, he is an artist as compared with priest or prophet elsewhere. Homer is an artist as distinct from a prophet, and yet he, with Hesiod, made the popular Greek religion. Here are the words of one of their own historians, Herodotus: 'Homer and Hesiod invented a theogony [or, as we should say, a theology] for the Greeks, and gave the gods their appropriate epithets.' And accordingly we have the now stale but most true remark that Homer was the Greek Bible, and did for the Greek people, politically and socially, some part of what the Bible has done for the nationality and culture of England. It is another example to show how in Greece the usual relations of Art and Religion are inverted, and Art gives to Religion more than she ever got from it except bare existence.

Historically and actually, then, Homer made the Greek religion which we know best. He gave it the form which it ever afterwards kept among the mass, and which was only purified, not banished, by subsequent artists. I have already referred to the criticism which Plato in the *Republic* exercised on Homeric theology (like modern criticism of early Old Testament ethics), and to the purified and exalted conception of the Homeric Zeus in the great statue of Phidias at Olympia. A similar service was done to Greek religion by the dramatists.

Before, however, enlarging on this, I venture to remind you that the drama itself was historically the offspring of religious worship. It is a long story, that of the development of Greek tragedy and comedy from the rude worship of the gods, and the festivities which accompanied it, to the stately argument of the great dramatic age. But there can be no doubt of the fact that this great child of art, like many artists also, had a most humble origin. It arose in the rural observances connected with two or three of the great deities, especially Dionysos. Here again, however, Art gives gold for brass, and for wood iron, and repays its parent for its origin a hundredfold.

GREEK ART AND RELIGION

I have hitherto spoken almost entirely of the Greek's love of Nature, and his power of entering into and setting forth her joy and beauty. But there was another element of the Greek mind which grew up alongside of that, and in the end had a most powerful effect upon it. I refer to the element of ethical seriousness—the moral element as distinct from the merely poetic and naturalistic. Greek thought was too penetrating not to see that there was an order in things beyond the order of Nature, and the Greek was too much of a politician not to perceive that the other and deeper order lay in the relations of man with man. The tendency in things which makes for righteousness, and which falls so heavily in the end on those who make for unrighteousness—that tendency the best Greeks knew as well as we do, and felt no less profoundly. This direction of thought, however powerful in Socrates and Plato, does not receive its most powerful expression till it is united with poetic art. The wedding takes place in the drama. Greek drama is the union of the ethical earnestness and the poetic art of Greece. And it may, therefore, be true to say that the dramatic poets in this land correspond, even more than its other artists, even its orators, to what the Hebrew prophet was in his, especially when we observe what artists in style and strophe these prophets were. It was the element of guilt, retribution, and purification in the old legends of the gods and heroes that the dramatists seized, and not the element of beauty. Æschylus is the grand and lurid apostle of a hereditary nemesis descending through generations from its source in a single act of insolence or sin. It is an ethical and atoned calm that is the crown of the Sophoclean drama. And with him no less than with Æschylus, the breach of the world's moral order in the soul is the source of general disaster and woe. The dramatic art in Greece, then, not only had a religious origin and a moral inspiration rising to religion of a very high sort, but it did religion the great service of purifying and ennobling it. And especially it drew public attention to the ethical order in the old conceptions, just as the sculptors had exalted the element of calm beauty and beneficent power. A time came when the sense of beauty failed the Greek in its highest form, but, to his woe, he did not quite lose this sense of moral law. It remained to torment him; and it received fresh fuel when the powerful Roman will and sense of order came in to condemn the disordered state of things. We have it conjoined with much beauty and wit in Aristophanes, with much wit, much horror, and no beauty, in Juvenal and Persius. We have then a form of art which these Romans carried to great perfection through the education the Greeks had given them in the art of expressing themselves. We have the unlovely moral protest harshly uttered by debased art in the face of a demoralised society. We have satire.

I draw to a close. I have indicated the peculiar and happy balance between spirit and Nature, soul and body, which marked the Greek genius,

GREEK ART AND RELIGION

and which is the note of Greek religion, the temper which is above all things healthy and sane, if neither tender nor profound. I have pointed out how this religion not only, as in the case of other faiths, ran into an artistic expression, but absolutely was absorbed into Art, and spoke through its artists as other creeds spoke through their priest, prophet, or saint. I have shown how Art took the place of Religion. It might also have been shown how this supremacy of Art over Religion became the final ruin of both, how the outward came to shape the inward instead of being shaped by it, and vengeance overtook this unnatural usurpation. Art for Art's sake did not keep Greece in the proud place which she took while she pursued Art for the sake of Religion. I have indicated the qualities of Greek art which naturally flowed from the Greek relation to Nature as those of calm, harmony, balance, perfectness of expression, and complete adequacy of material utterance for the soul. That soul was a limited one in many respects, but, such as it was, it had the happy fate of finding fit and complete expression. It was measured, but never tongue-tied. And in this respect I might have alluded to the great perfection of the Greeks in the art of oratory. I have also glanced at the actual and historical, as distinct from the philosophical, connection of this religion and this art. I have said their very mythology—the most beautiful in existence—was a work of art. I have indicated architecture, sculpture, poetry, all as emerging from the cradle of Religion, and poetry especially becoming the vehicle of the Greek moral earnestness raised to a religious intensity.

But it has probably occurred to you that I have had nothing to say about two great departments of art which, more than either architecture or sculpture, absorb our modern genius and our modern interest. I mean the arts of music and painting.

These did exist among the Greeks, but they existed in a degree of perfection far below that reached by the other arts. We know less, to be sure, about Greek music and Greek painting, because these are arts that are not embodied in a permanent material, and the further art of multiplying copies on a large scale was unknown. But the great proof of the low condition of these arts among this people is the small enthusiasm expressed for them by its writers. There are causes contained in the nature of these arts themselves for their comparative neglect among a people like the Greeks, causes which are intimately associated with religious considerations, and which are to be sought in the defects of Greek religion. These arts, as we shall see later, express and touch a region of the soul which to the Greek was very unfamiliar, if not unknown. They embarked him on the open sea. They took him (to speak in a figure) out of his familiar Mediterranean, and sent him beyond the Pillars of Hercules with his prow to the spiritual infinite. And no compass for that region was as yet in his hands. There was something in human destiny waiting to be ex-

GREEK ART AND RELIGION

pressed which the Greek knowledge of the natural man had not yet discovered, and which the bright Greek consciousness, even in its disorder, but dimly surmised. The depths of the Christian soul, with its subtle and changing lights, its fine lines and delicate structures, its profound passion, tumult and solemnity — these make a region of things from which there came to the Greek only bodings of perplexity and dread. He had no chart of that land; therefore he exercised his happy power of turning away from it, of putting it aside; and he ran from that dim, mysterious aisle—full, as we now see it, of such solemn and powerful beauty—into the broad sunlight of the more congenial and superficial moods. It was when men, led by the hand of God, grew used to the world which lay beyond the Greek's glad earth, when they had acquired a new power of seeing in the dark, drinking from the flinty rock, and extracting both power and beauty from sin, sorrow, and death—it was then that Greek art with its finite perfection was felt inadequate for the vastness of the new world and the depth of the new spirit. And it was then that music and painting came to the fore. These arts were found to be capable of suggesting at once human yearning and human rest with the Infinite, as the Greek, satisfied with the finite, never could. The plastic arts you may call the arts of the finite. It was from a finite religion they sprang and throve. But music and painting are the arts of the Infinite. They consort with the religion of the Infinite, and they express its romantic deepening of the human soul. They give voice, not to its happy health, but to the quivering gamut of human sorrow, or to the joy of absorption into the infinite love and pity of God.

> Infinite pity, and the pain
> Of finite hearts that yearn.

In a word, infinite, holy Love had entered the world, and man had to find a new speech for his new heart. It spoke in painting and in music. Greek art, says Ruskin most truly, is the product of a time when the best minds were discussing the nature of Justice, Italian art of a time when they were discussing the nature of Justification.

There was one great picture in ancient Greece about which we know, from the reports and descriptions of those who had seen or heard of it, and from a sketch of it on the walls of a house in Pompeii. It is the work of a painter called Timanthes, and represents the sacrifice of Iphigenia when the oracle had declared that her death was needful to free the windbound fleet of Greece, and speed the national enterprise against Troy. The spectators and friends stand round the victim with various degrees of grief and pity depicted in their faces. Chief among these is her father Agamemnon. But the painter has covered his face with his hand in his robe. This device has given rise to a vast amount of criticism, both in ancient and modern times, some admiring it as a consummate stroke, others despising it as a

GREEK ART AND RELIGION

mere trick of evasive art. Various have been the reasons assigned for it. The artist, some say, had in the other faces exhausted his own power of portraying grief, and it was beyond him to depict the father's agony. No, say others, it was not the artist, but the art that was weak. It is not in the power of art in any hands to exhibit worthily a father's woe in such a case. Wrong still, says a third. It is not an evidence of weakness either in the artist or the art. It is within the power of an artist who is a master of his art to paint the emotion even of that awful moment. But it is an evidence of the artist's true Greek strength and self-control, his true Greek sense of the proper limitations of Art. He would attempt to do only what the stringent and dominant law of Beauty would allow his art to do. Art could represent it, but it would be with such a contortion of feature and strain of agony that the horror of it would destroy the dominant beauty, and reduce the work below the level of worthy Art. It would have lost the lofty calm and the noble beauty which were indispensable to the Greek idea of art, and especially to a situation so grand.

Probably enough, this last is the true explanation of the painter's motive. But yet Christendom has been worshipping the beauty of such a sacrifice raised to a far vaster scale. 'He that spared not His own Son, but freely gave Him up to the death for us all.' Has that ideal been one whose revelation to the soul of Christendom has filled it with horror and revolt? The very contrary.

This belief has been the source of inspiration for some of the highest flights that pictorial art has reached. But what does that mean? It means that the human idea of Beauty has been altered and enlarged. It has been moralised by the beauty of holiness. We still insist that Art must be beautiful, but we give a wider scope to Beauty through a new treatment of sorrow, and a deeper significance for Love. We have expanded the whole modern canon of what beauty is, through the Christian beauty of holy, saving sorrow. But none the less the new beauty was impossible without the old. Greece was one of the schoolmasters that bring us to Christ, the joyful forerunner of one greater than herself. Her message is not yet ended. And Art still learns from her ancient glories, as from no other source, lessons to apply on an infinitely larger and profounder scale.

III

HEBREW ART AND RELIGION

THE second commandment passes the death sentence on Hebrew art. In killing idolatry, it killed plastic imagination. At least it placed it under such a disadvantage that it could hardly live, and certainly could not grow. So little was God, among this people, a projection of the inward man, that every such creation on man's part was jealously watched, and promptly nipped. Neither painter, sculptor, nor dramatist could live under the shadow of this stern law, or in the midst of this grimly earnest people. Such is the complaint of both Philo and Origen in speaking of the Jews.[1]

It was not without remonstrance on the part of some of the Jews themselves that this law was carried out as vigorously as it was. Sharing human nature as they did after all, it was impossible but that some among them should hanker for expansion into the beautiful and ideal world which forms the atmosphere of Art. But these humaner spirits were silenced, or all but silenced, by the pressure of the national genius, and the mission of the national calling. It was in

[1] We have the same prohibition in the Koran and the same result in Islam; to say nothing of Scotland. English Puritanism was different.

vain that some of them contended that the prohibition in this commandment was not aimed at objects of art, but only of idolatry. We may see clearly enough that the whole context and spirit of the commandment justified them in so construing it. But it was not so seen by the mass of the people; and it was less and less seen as they grew older, more exclusive, and more literal in their reading of the law. We may contend if we like—it was urged also by the more liberal Jews of old—that Moses himself allowed a certain amount of representative art, and that it entered largely into the decoration of both Tabernacle and Temple. We may point to the graven cherubim in the holiest place. We are answered, ' These are but symbols. They are not likenesses of anything actually existent in heaven or earth. And, moreover, they are where nobody sees them but the High Priest once a year.' We may point again to the carved flowers, and fruits, and trees that adorned the friezes and capitals of the Temple, to the gorgeous figured hangings that decorated both Tabernacle and Temple; to the brazen serpent itself; to the twelve brazen bulls that supported in the Temple court the great brazen sea; to the gold and ivory lions on the steps of Solomon's throne; to many such things we may point. It was wrong elsewhere, nevertheless, said the thoroughgoing Jew. It was illegal, said the pure Pharisee, speaking through Josephus. It was idolatry, or leading to it. We must have no more of it. And very little more of it they did have. It is possible,

HEBREW ART AND RELIGION

though not probable, that they misunderstood the commandment, and the critics to-day could have put matters right. But none the less do they indicate in an extreme form the spirit and temper of the nation, the spirit from which the commandment itself proceeded even when it did not go so far. Representative Art was all but banished from the service of Religion. In its highest forms it was entirely banished. It was discouraged by Religion. And the result was that it never really came into existence. So close is the connection between Religion and Art. I have already illustrated the closeness of that connection by the contrary case. We have seen how the genius of Greek religion developed into Art—not only encouraged it, but put itself wholly into it—and the result was the most perfect Art the world has seen. The artistic position of the Hebrews establishes the same connection from the negative side. Here was a religion which, on the whole, frowned on Art, and, as a consequence, Art never among that people took being. So that a lecture on Hebrew Art is like the chapter on lions in Norway. There is no Hebrew Art. We have some traces of Egyptian symbolism. We have a music of which we know little, but can guess that it was more loud than lovely. It was semi-barbaric like the profuse and loud hangings of the Temple. And the Temple itself is said to have been little larger than a good parish church, and was the work of foreign artists. The second Temple, of course, showed the influences of Babylon, and the third those of Greece.

But my subject is not Art, but Religion and Art. It becomes of moment, therefore, to examine the causes, both direct and indirect, which determined this faith in a direction so contrary to the tendency of religion in general, and the Greek religion in particular.

There are three classes of consideration which explain the æsthetic barrenness of Israel.

1. The nature of the religion.
2. The native character and genius of the race.
3. The history of the people and their circumstances.

1. *The Nature of the Religion*

In dealing with this people, we deal with an entirely different race from those whose spiritual condition I have traced. I spoke in the first lecture, you may recollect, about the various and advancing stages achieved by the human spirit in relation to Nature, and I took, as examples of the spiritual rise and progress of man's soul, India, Egypt, and Greece. From the subjection of spirit to Nature in India, we traced the first assertions of spiritual independence in Egypt, on to the balance and equality of spirit with Nature in Greece. But these peoples belong to an ethnological family very different in its spiritual characters from the race we have now to deal with. Leaving out of view the question of Egyptian ethnology, India and Greece belong to the Indo-European family, while Israel belongs to the Semitic family. The former includes the people of India, Persia, Greece,

HEBREW ART AND RELIGION 47

Rome, Germany, and all the west of Europe. The latter includes the Assyrians, the Phœnicians, the Jews (and the neighbouring tribes of Moabites, Philistines, etc., whom the Jews continually fought), the Arabs, the Ethiopians, and the Carthaginians. We are able, chiefly by means of the scientific interpretation of language, of their oldest and commonest words, to get at the fundamental religious conception of these two great families or races, and we find that these are exceedingly distinct. It was at one time common to say that they differed religiously in this, that the Indo-Europeans were polytheistic while the Semites were the grand monotheists of antiquity. But a glance at the Semitic cults outside Israel is enough to destroy our faith in a general Semitic monotheism. It was not Indo-European idolatry that the Jews inclined to, and the prophets so fiercely denounced. It was the Semitic idolatries from which Israel itself had emerged, and to which it had racial affinities and congenital attractions in the way of reversion to type. The worship of Assyria was polytheist. The worship of Philistia was idolatrous. No pantheon was more populous than the Phœnician, and no people were ever more catholic and comprehensive in their additions to it. Mahomet found the Arabians polytheists, and the monotheism of the Ethiopians has not made a conspicuous mark on history. Hence, merely to call the Semites monotheists off-hand, and the Indo-Europeans polytheists, does not meet the facts of the case. Let us go inward from the outward worships or imaginative pantheons. Let us take the idea of God, the idea of the divine power, as distinct from specific conceptions of it, or imaginative embodiments of it. That is the ultimate question to be asked about a religion, What is its idea of God? Now, applying this question to the two races aforesaid, and seeking the answer in that oldest repository of thought, viz. language, we do find a great difference, one which may lead to monotheism on the one hand, or to polytheism on the other, but which is not the same as either. Not to go too deeply into the matter, we find that the oldest names of God in the Indo-European family are drawn from the powers or the phenomena of Nature. They are naturalistic religion. In the Semitic family, on the other hand, the greatest names of God are drawn from the human consciousness, the spirit, and express moral or metaphysical qualities and relations. The great God of the Indo-Europeans, the Greek Zeus, draws his name and origin from the clear, shining heavens (Dyaus in Sanskrit is the clear sky); even the great God of the Semitic peoples is either El the strong, the mighty one, or Bel Baal = Lord, master, husband; Jahve Himself was originally a Nature God. But the latent genius of the chosen race emerges in the moral qualities He comes to wear. In the one case a natural object; in the other, a moral or metaphysical idea takes command. Now, which religion is more likely to be monotheistic? Well, to answer that, ask further where does the primitive, active, and undisciplined man find most unity? In Nature or in himself? without or within his own consciousness? Why, clearly in himself. His *self*, or his sept, is the one thing he is sure of, and which he will fight and work for. The variety of Nature perplexes and confuses him. He is ready with a new God for each of its new forces. But he himself, or his chief, is a force that he dimly but powerfully feels to be one. Therefore, it is in the Semitic religions that we find the monotheistic germ, and amid all the multitude of Semitic gods we can say (what we cannot say of those of the other races) that the idea, the conception, is the same. The difference is only in name or in locality. The thought was the same. And it was based on personality and personal relations. The Semites had not the Indo-European tendency to resolve God into an abstraction, an essence, an impersonal nature-force expressed in terms of imagination or thought. We find in the Semites the pantheon neither of India nor of Greece.

The Indo-Europeans began with Nature; they were therefore committed to development. Mind had to rise gradually to the assertion of its place in relation to Nature. The Semites, on the other hand, began from within. They began with Mind or Soul. Nature was but the product of Spirit, its creation, its tool. Where the Hindoos placed the vastness of Nature, the Hebrews placed the vastness of a spiritual power. In both, indeed, we have the Oriental bias towards the colossal. But in India it remains only the colossal; whereas in

Israel it becomes the true sublime. In both cases the vastness lay as a weight on the human spirit. In India the spirit of man was crushed into deformity or impotence by huge Nature. In Israel the human spirit was crushed into abasement or awe. In neither could it have a perfectly free development. In India it was crushed by the alien power of Nature. But in Israel it was crushed by a power kindred to its own, the divine spirit, which was all the more powerful because it was kindred, and could search and know the trembling soul of man. But in the fact of the kinship lay a developing force as well. The dread of the divine spirit was terrible; but it was not all dread, because not all foreign. In the essence of the conception lay the fact of moral relationship to the divine. He was Lord, Master, even Husband. He could speak to them in their moral speech. Hence they could hope and aspire, not to equal him indeed, but at least to know him, to share his thought, his regard, and, above all, his covenant. The Greek was continuous with Nature, but the Hebrew was its *vis-à-vis* created by Spirit, and secured by a covenant.

In relation to Nature, then, the human mind took two directions, one in each of these great races. To reach an equality with Nature, the Indo-European spirit had to ascend from beneath it, but the Semitic spirit had to descend from above it. The first, therefore, found Nature more or less capable and worthy of expressing soul. The second seldom found such capacity or worth in Nature. It moved in the region of the supernatural, and saw things which it was not possible for flesh and blood to utter. The first consequently had a splendid or a perfect art. The second had no art, in the strict sense of the word, but an unearthly faith.

This applies to all the Semitic peoples in different degrees. They had no art of their own at all. They borrowed, they imitated, and they frequently spoiled good art in the transfer. The Assyrians borrowed from Babylon, the Phœnicians borrowed from Egypt; but art of their own they had little or none.

Art was not the task which fell to this family in the division of the world's work. Theirs was a still higher and a more precious heritage. It was theirs, in one small but immortal branch of them, to develop and to maintain the true ethical spirituality, which involves the unity, of God. It was theirs to teach us, once and for ever, that God dwelleth not in temples made with hands, and is not worshipped with things of man's device, that the shrine and commerce of God are in the soul, that He is spiritually discerned, that He is to be set forth in righteousness, that neither our handiwork, nor our imagination, nor our intellectual conception, can be more than symbols, they are hardly revelations, of One whose grace is more than His essence or His presence. It was theirs to nurse and transmit that exalted and spiritual conception of the highest which, if it impoverished the world in one way, enriched it vastly more in another, and if it straitened its geniality in many ways, yet gave it its release into the joy unspeakable and full of glory. It was theirs to be shaken, rent, and abased by the spiritual consciousness of God, till every human faculty felt uncertain of itself, and natural grace was lost in the strain of inspiration and the volume of revelation. As the seer put his hand on his mouth and his mouth in the dust before the purity of God, so was silenced and abased the faculty of plastic utterance in the whole people. To what will ye liken me, saith the Holy One of Israel. That plastic, representative power was so continually reminded of its utter inadequacy, reminded in tones of pity, of scorn, of mockery, of command, and of entire prohibition, that it never took courage to lift its head and live. The whole world was but the footstool of God. Was it worth while to spend energy upon the decoration of a footstool, or the contemplation of its beauty? The footstool was sacred indeed, but not in itself. Only because the Almighty had trodden it underfoot. It might become the reminder, or the symbol, of Him; it could never represent Him, when even the Heaven of Heavens could not contain Him. Semitism had, therefore, none of those delicacies of perception or those sympathetic intimacies so indispensable for art, no shades of spiritual life, *nuances* of suggestion, or degrees of its existence and progress. They owned the spiritual more than they understood it. They had not the fine perception of the soul which comes of love and its Christian sight.

This overwhelming vastness of the divine in the East—the colossal of India, the sublime of Israel—is the cause of the specific form of Oriental art. It is symbolical art, as distinguished from representative, from the classical art of Greece or the romantic art of Christianity. 'Thou art so far,' is the devotional utterance of the East, which therefore hints at the divine in symbol. 'Thou art so near,' was the Greek's address to his gods, and he gives perfect shape to the divine in a human form. It is Christianity that boldly and reverently says at once, 'Thou art so near and yet so far'; and hence Christianity at once speaks in Art and controls it. To the Eastern, and especially to the Semite, adequate expression and clear utterance of the divine was impossible. It was too overwhelming. And such expression was equally impossible, whether the medium was æsthetic form or mere language. He could but hint at his God. He could not represent Him. It was the symbolism of association, not of resemblance. It is easy for Nature worshippers to be artists, because it is easy to represent the objects of Nature. But for a religion of the Semitic and spiritual type it is otherwise. In the first place, there is the majesty of the deity, which depresses Art with hopelessness, because all representation is but so many shades of inadequacy, or degrees of finitude. In the second place, where the divine is expressed, not through natural objects, but through spiritual qualities and moral relations, their representation is impossible. You cannot have a representation of a relation or of a moral quality. What representation could there be of the idea Jehovah, the self-existent? The artist or literary nature scorns the Absolute as a piece of drab theory. So in despair of representation, Art became only symbolic or suggestive. It remained in an adult infancy. Hence we have the various symbols of the Semitic faiths—mere hints or suggestions—adjectives attached to the deity, as it were, not names. We have the winged bull, the man lion, the winged globe, in Assyria, and the cherubim, the ark, the brazen serpent, in Israel. Upon these the thought did not tarry. It was not tempted to tarry. They were not platforms, but steps in the ascent to God—footstools, like the whole world. They expressed but a quality, not the whole deity. They but suggested the divine. They were pegs on which to hang religious reflection, reminders, intimations. But they were neither expressions nor manifestations of the whole God. And they were not, and could not be, worshipped.

And it is to simple symbolic objects after all that Religion most readily attaches itself. They give no shock to the spirit of reverence by an unseemly effort to represent the unspeakably holy, and their humility of suggestion is their virtue for revelation. The daubs of the Virgin or Christ have drawn more genuine devotion round them, and do still in Catholic countries, than the great masterpieces of Art. More has been done for the spirit of true religion by the simple symbol of the Cross than by all the Crucifixions ever painted.

HEBREW ART AND RELIGION

And hymns, poor as poetry, serve faith as the finest poetry cannot do.

These Semitic tendencies came to the surface in but one branch of the race—the Hebrews. And among them it was only in the most choice and exalted spirits that they found clear utterance. So far, however, as their testimony goes, its object is to remove God as far as possible from Nature while yet deepening His connection and control. No grove, for instance, was allowed closely to surround the Temple. No part of Nature was ever regarded as a part or an embodiment of God. The utmost it could do was to bear witness from afar, to be a symbol, not an incarnation, of the divine. The Incarnation is not a Hebrew, but an Indo-European idea. Redemption is Hebrew, but not Incarnation.

It is quite true that the Jews used very bold and anthropomorphic expressions about God. He snorts in anger. He repents. He smells a sweet savour. He comes down, talks, and even eats with man. He rides on a cherub. He has shield and spear. But it is well understood that these are but figurative modes of speech, and many of them belong to the literature and conceptions of an early age, when the influence of the old idolatries still remained and current modes of speech yet bore traces of them. In the later and more monotheistic ages, in the mouth of the great prophets, for instance, we find little such imagery. The communication with God is conducted in the recesses of the spirit, and with the solemnity of the unseen. And it is a remarkable paradox that these anthropomorphic expressions vanished in proportion as the sympathy between God and man was more deeply realised. The prophets, who use none of them, are they who feel most keenly the human sympathy of God. Anthropomorphism is not sympathy. As they came to realise more deeply the kindness of God to man's highest part, they ceased to use language implying His community in the lower. And this in particular is to be noted in Jewish anthropomorphism—God was never reduced to a man. The body was but worn as a garment, or used for a purpose. It was felt to be impossible to embody God fully or permanently in human form or speech. This was an impossibility which, we said, the Greek did not feel. In the religion of Israel, then, there is neither the thoroughgoing anthropomorphism nor the pantheism of Greece. And as these must be elements of a religion which sets strongly towards Art, the religion of Israel was therefore not artistic. It was holy. And while the good, the beautiful, the true may all find some more or less complete and visible embodiment, the holy never can. It is spiritual, and spiritual alone.

And to all time this Jewish people will live, because it is to them we owe the triumphant assertion of the moral spirituality of the divine, and the worthlessness, in comparison, of every embodiment of God, whether in art, or creed, or institution. Those have but a relative, not an absolute, validity. Measured against this transcendent height and light, all our conceptions are but symbols indeed, stepping-stones, ladders between earth and heaven. Our best thoughts of Him, as thoughts only, are little more than degrees of darkness; our highest powers but grades of impotence. Still, it is His light that makes our darkness visible. It is His power that makes us feel even our own impotence. And it is of His own ordinance that we find, in the things which we see and make, symbols and faint similitudes of Him.

2. *The Nature of the People*

The second class of considerations explaining the Hebrew barrenness in Art is drawn from the peculiar genius and character of the people.

There was little that was ideal, in the strict sense of the word, about this people. They had bright visions of an ideal future, but into the ideal world which accompanies the present they did not enter. They were not persecuted or inspired by the sense of unearthly beauty, and they had no power of dealing with abstractions. The power of continuous thought was not theirs, and they could not follow out a complex whole into its parts, or set them all forth in due subordination to the whole. That is to say, they had no sense of organic unity. This is a defect which is quite fatal to the prospects of great Art anywhere. One of the first requirements of a work of high Art is that it should be a sort of economy or organism. Every part must contribute to a general and central idea, which pervades the whole, vivifies it, and furnishes a reason for its existence. Every portion must contribute something to the general idea. If there be anything which does not so contribute —if in a drama there be an act or a character which lags superfluous on the stage, and does not forward in some way the action of the piece—that is inartistic. It must, in the first-rate art, be pruned away. The most perfect natural object of this kind is the human body. And it was the representation of this which naturally absorbed the energies of the most perfect art, the art of sculpture in Greece. But this power the Hebrew had not. Look at his art, his temple. What was it in point of design? Nothing more, it has been said, than an aggregate of cells, a number of apartments mostly square, heaped together without any central, artistic design, and with the architectural poverty covered by profuse and barbaric decoration. What was his way of writing history? Simply the narration of episode after episode round the national idea—mere annalism, with no *provenance* and no pragmatism—so devoid of any artistic unity of form or design that editors could add or subtract freely, or fuse up the material into new shape, without any offence. There is, indeed, strophic structure of a kind in the Psalms. But the longest psalm in the book is, as regards structure, not a work of art at all. It is an acrostic, and is composed of sentence after sentence—each true, good, and even fine—but forming in the aggregate no artistic unity, and ruled by no central and shaping idea, only by a devout mood. These examples

HEBREW ART AND RELIGION 59

will show what is meant when we say that the Hebrew genius worked, not by way of developing a central idea through the parts in harmonious beauty, but by adding part to part, or plaiting them in, till the result was not an organism, but an aggregate, or a stratification. Art works by evolution. They worked by accretion. All the arts of form therefore, those which depend on balance and proportion, were impossible to them. I ought, however, to say that in the prophecies, especially the later ones, there are efforts made with some success after a certain structure, balance, and proportion, which would almost suggest foreign influence of some kind. And in the Song of Solomon and the Book of Job we have a still more distinct effort after artistic form. These are the only Hebrew writings in which artistic form of a real kind is an object held in view, and they are comparatively late.

Hebrew art is almost entirely literary and poetic; and even there it is less conscious than unconscious art. It is the simple, spontaneous art of Burns, not the cultured, elaborated art of Tennyson. If the Hebrews could not grasp or follow a complex whole, they had a vigorous power of seizing upon individual phases of feeling or of Nature. The Hebrew imagination was quick, mobile, and realistic, not calm, intuitive, and constructive. They were a passionate, direct, and strong-willed people, who regarded the world entirely in relation to their own place in it. They could not examine it at arm's-length, so to speak. They never thought how it would look in a picture, or how it might be scientifically expressed. They had neither pictorial taste nor scientific curiosity. It was a personal, not a theoretical standard they had for things. Their religion, you remember, was one based on personality, on personal qualities and relations. They had no theories of the universe. It was all the result of the fiat of a supreme will. There is a theology, and above all a teleology, but no system, in the Old Testament. They did not desire to examine the concatenation of things, but their destination. What are now called secondary causes had for them no existence. Everything was the immediate result of a will, and everything had a purpose. This will and this purpose it was the business of their great spokesman, the prophet, to see and foresee, and to expound them with all the resources of an oratory more full of force than balance.

Their faith being so purely spiritual, they were committed, if to any part at all, to the most spiritual and least sensuous of all the arts, namely poetry. But within the poetic sphere, their genius being quick, passionate, ready to link individual aspects of Nature and individual moods of feeling, it was in lyric poetry that they could most successfully speak. The lyric utterance of profound religious emotion—that is the greatest contribution they have made to Art. They gave the world its great religious hymns. Now that may be a small thing in respect of Art. Hymns are not high art. They are not odes. But they make a priceless thing in respect of Religion. These lyrics are the passionate utterances each of a single spiritual experience, in several moods or phases, with a movement of ascent, beginning often in despair to end in triumph, or in prayer to end in praise. These emotions are mixed with rapid, vivid visions of Nature—glances of sight rather than flashes of insight—with beautiful associations, rather than harmonies, of the outward world with the inward mood; but we have no pictures for the picture's sake. The poet does not aim at a composition where the natural objects should all be in mutual keeping. It is enough for him if they are so far harmonious with his own emotion as to help him to express it with intensity or beauty. He is not busied chiefly with his production. He is busy chiefly with his profound reality of emotion. For that the earth is his footstool. And illustrating Wordsworth's law of poetic diction, he pours out his soul in the simplest, strongest, and directest language, the language of the common people, and the imagery of the common, but perennially impressive, aspects of Nature.

It is clear that this is not the attitude towards Nature which gives birth to great art. For that purpose the imagination must be detained by Nature. It must lovingly dwell upon it, follow it, wait upon it, understand it, for its own sake. Now that is just what the Hebrew did not, and could not do. It has been said by Hegel, ' Nature among this people was undeified, but not yet understood.' Israel had glimpses of Nature, glimpses which left her less forlorn, but she did not wind her way by patient love into the secret place where Nature's loveliness has its abode. It was not in the Hebrew genius to consider the lilies. And when it essayed to consider the heavens, it was not in and for themselves, but as the work of God's finger, ' the sun and moon which Thou hast ordained '; and it is, moreover, only to turn immediately to the reflection, ' What is man that Thou art mindful of him ? ' But then this incapacity, which made great art impossible, saved them from that immersion in Nature which was the vice of Oriental religion and the source of its worst idolatries. If Israel did not extract the sweetest of Nature's honey, she yet avoided the fate of the drunken bee which sips the poppied syrup till in the charmed and fatal calyx it sinks, drowned. And we may indicate in one word the difference between Greece and Israel in respect of Nature. The Greek idealised it, and dwelt on it. The Hebrew spiritualised it, and passed beyond it.

3. *The Country and History of the People*

I come now to deal with the third class of considerations which stunted Jewish art. There were some artistic germs in Israel, but they were not clamorous for scope. And they were sterilised by the puritans of that lofty faith, and scorched by the scirocco of the prophetic soul. But there were also circumstances, both in the features of the

HEBREW ART AND RELIGION

country and in the vicissitudes of their history, which exercised a fatal influence on Hebrew art.

(1) As to the effect of natural features. The Semitic races were the inhabitants of a portion of the world where Nature was much more difficult, distant, and inhospitable than in a land like Greece. They had to wrest their subsistence from the arid soil, they were fringed by barren deserts and waste, howling wildernesses. Nature did not reach them a friendly hand, or invite them by much grace of manner to familiarity, or even hospitality. Whether to the eye or the hand of man, she offered little to enrapture or to engage. The vast mountains and the long dreary steppes of the Semitic region are just the features to oppress man with the sense of the Infinite, and with a feeling of his own impotence to tame the world to his use or his art. What a part the desert plays in the Bible—like the part the sea plays with us. Human thought in solitudes like these, especially the thought of a nomadic people, wandered forth, unstayed by the seductions of a diversified surface, into the contemplation of a world beyond the world. As the early Semite gazed across the desert, or looked to the top of a bleak hill, there was nothing to fascinate his fancy or to catch the garment of his spirit. There was only footing, as it were, from which to mount to heaven; and the horizon, or the hilltop, was but a step in man's approach to the Eternal, or a footstool for the Eternal in his descent to man.

How different it was in Greece! The clear,

bright sunshine of a land surrounded, pierced, and cooled by the sea took the place of the desert's torrid noon. The Greek could enjoy the daylight, and he learned to love the finite beauty that the sunshine reveals. But the Semite must live in the shade during the day. It was at night that he came out to enjoy the beauty of the world. But the beauty of night is the beauty of the Infinite. Earthly things lose both colour and form. The things of heaven grow more deep and clear. Thought is repelled from earth, and cast to the sky. The formless majesty of the rolling heavens subdues the soul, hushes the self-assertion of its creative powers, and quenches at its spring the bare suggestion of imitative representation, of Art. It was there, in that illimitable and unfathomable blue of night, that it behoved the Eternal, the Divine, to dwell, not in the narrow suggestions of the garish day, or in the objects of the light as reflected in the cunning handiwork of men. Then again, in Greece the country was small and diversified. It was watered by many a stream, and cut up in many a cleft. 'The sunshine in the happy glens was fair.' The people were not oppressed with the sense of the world's inhospitable vastness. It was a fertile and happy clime, more adapted for the culture of the graces than of the sterner virtues and fidelities of life. The exquisite beauty of plain after plain, of vale behind vale, hill upon hill, and stream beside stream, did invite the thoughts to tarry before they left earth behind, or trod it underfoot in the

HEBREW ART AND RELIGION

ascent to heaven. A thousand lovely hands caught at the garment of the soul, and said, Stay with us. Even as men looked across the waters, it was not an infinite sea on which they gazed. Their thought of the Infinite was broken up and distributed among the numberless islands that adorned the bosom of the Ægean. And the habits of the people were not nomadic, but settled. They learned, by early and long familiarity with a small spot of Nature's face, that love, sympathy, and understanding of her which is so much for Art. The city, too, the fixed centre of the settled and civilised life—it was worth while decorating that. It was not a place which was exposed to the ravages of barbarian conquerors, nor a place which they exhausted of substance, and then passed on to fresh woods and new pastures. It would remain for their children. It was ordered and fenced, secure against violence from the mob within or from the foe without.

The Hebrews in Palestine possessed a country somewhat less dreary than the wastes and plains that were peopled by the other Semitic tribes, a country a little like Greece in variety of feature and beauty of surface. But the genius of the people was much shaped by the conditions of their nomadic forefathers in the wider East. And there were, in the particular case of Israel, historic circumstances which were enough in themselves to destroy even a stronger artistic bias than they ever revealed. There was an absence of that settled serenity which was so kind to art in Greece.

I will mention some of those circumstances which tended to discourage art apart from the religion and apart from the specific genius of the people.

(2) The history of the nation is a succession of the very conditions that kill Art. Art requires rest—some ease of condition and circumstance, some established and guaranteed position, some security from sudden and disastrous change, so much control over Nature and man as shall rid the people of deep anxiety about the meaner needs of life, and free them to contemplate life in its higher and calmer aspects. Such a period never occurred in the history of Israel. In its first period the nation was engaged in a taxing struggle to gain a national footing and a recognised place among the peoples around. That was secured at last under David, and under Solomon it seemed as if for this people also a life of art and culture was among the possibilities. But immediately there followed the disruption of the realm, and some centuries of what may well enough be called civil war. Before these were over, both the kingdoms had come into collision with the great eastern empires of Babylon and Assyria; and before very much longer their national existence was taken away, and they underwent the purgation of the Captivity. When they returned, they had suffered too much to have any taste for Art. Clearly it was not their vocation. A greater task was laid on them, one nearer their genius. Their energy took mainly a religious direction. And it now took the direction of a religion free neither

in the prophetic nor the artistic sense, the religion of a ceremonial and priestly faith, where much of the soul was entangled in ritual, and the freedom germane to culture was replaced by the letter of meticulous conduct and ingenious casuistry. It is true also that the sense of sin and the problem of evil deepened in Judaism. Prophetism died, yet the people on the whole perhaps grew more serious. Theology widened and deepened with the sense of the intractability of guilt, in preparation for a greater product than Art. It was not in a history like that that Art could grow, or even live. The people of sorrow, like the Man of Sorrows, had no energy to spare for Art. And they had another call. They had a baptism to be baptized with, and how were they straitened till it should be accomplished. And the joy, when it came, was of a cast too holy to bear artistic form.

(3) Add to this troubled history the unkindness of earth and heaven in the frequent natural calamities falling upon a people with no economic system—the droughts, famines, locusts, which from time to time devastated industry, sowed despair, disease, and death in the nation, and gave to the spirit of the survivors a tone of grim and hard conflict with Nature not likely to issue in any loving reflection of her in Art.

(4) The form of government, moreover, was hostile to Art. Much has been said, and is to be said, as to the influence of democracy on Art. But the effect produced on it by the free republics of Greece, and in later times of Northern Italy, is

very different from that proceeding from what may be called the Tory democracies of old Rome or the French Second Empire. And the government of Israel was more nearly a Tory democracy than a free republic. It was neither a despotism nor a constitutional monarchy. It was the alliance of the 'Monarch and the Multitude,' revived by a latter-day Semite. In Empires like Assyria, Babylon, and Egypt, where the king was absolute, vast works of architectural art were undertaken and carried out. Prince took up what prince laid down, and the vanity or ambition of the reigning family used remorselessly the toil of the masses to perpetuate the fame of the dynasty in huge buildings or public works. But in Israel this was not possible. The people had too direct and close a power over the ruler. The crown, devoid of any envelope of constitutional forms, was placed in immediate contact with a people whose instincts were free. Prerogative met freedom, and its dignity suffered by the collision. It was impossible for the Hebrew rulers to undertake great works like the more despotic princes. For even if the people were silent, a great popular organ was always at hand—representing partly the Roman tribune, partly the modern press— I mean the prophet. He was always there, to prune the king's vanity, to divert him from reliance on visible power or temporal pomp, and to protest, in the name of the spiritual God, against everything which would remove confidence from the Lord of Hosts, or body forth the Holy One of

HEBREW ART AND RELIGION

Israel. It was in the prophets, and not the priests, that the distinctive genius, power, and call of Israel spoke forth. It was they that entered the great protests against representations of the divine. It was the prophets, embodying the purest spirit of the Semite, and exercised by the salutary dread of idolatry, that ploughed a preservative salt into the fields of the plastic imagination, and nipped the shoots of sprouting art. And they left to the world, in their impassioned protests against the sensuous imagination, our chief classics of the spiritual imagination.

(5) Again, we find in Israel no commemoration of the dead. And hence we find none of those splendid tombs which elsewhere offered such scope and encouragement to architectural and other art. The belief in immortality (except in dim Sheol) did not exist among the Jews till after the Captivity. The prevailing idea was that the good were duly rewarded by God in this life, either in themselves or their families, and that a sumptuous tomb would be a presumptuous addition of the survivors. The memory of the individual was especially transmitted by the existence of his family with their carefully kept genealogies; and the feeling of reverence for ancestors, while it never became worship, was strong enough to dispense with visible memorials furnished by an artist foreign to the family and the name.

(6) Consider also the effect on Art of the Temple at Jerusalem. It gave Art a certain impulse, but it did it harm in the end. The building of the

Temple was resisted and deferred as long as possible by the prophetic party. They would not allow David to do it. They had a true feeling, not only that it would encourage the artistic representation of the spiritual, but that it would have the effect of localising, and thereby impoverishing, the true, spiritual, and ubiquitous worship of God. There is no doubt it did have this effect. It was a rallying point for a kind of priestliness, which in the end is as fatal to pure art as to pure religion. And the fact that it became unique, that it became the only acceptable place for sacrifice and all the high ritual of Jewish worship, prevented the erection elsewhere of other temples to be fields for the exercise of such art as there was. We may estimate its effect in this way by trying to conceive what Greek art would have been if it had been confined to one temple alone at Athens, and the artistic spirit jealously watched and curbed even there.

(7) And lastly, let it be borne in mind that the Israelites were then an agricultural people, not a commercial, and they did not gather in the huge masses which indicate a ripe civilisation and rear a fine art. There was a rusticity about their ideas of life which smacked of the vineyard and the reaping field, and which appeared with great charm and sweetness in their domestic life. But it did not impel them towards Art. Their Tabernacle was but an Arab tent enlarged and embellished, and the Temple followed the principle. They did not grave their history in an ambitious

HEBREW ART AND RELIGION

way upon such monuments of stone and metal as have handed down to us the records of Egypt or Greece. The handicrafts which form the mechanical basis of Art were not in their line. They were not artisans, and it may be partly for that reason that they were not artists. They did recognise with an admirable catholicity the Divine Spirit as the inspiration of cunning craftsmen like Bezaleel and Aholiab, ' wise-hearted men in whom the Lord put wisdom and understanding to know how to work all manner of work for the service of the sanctuary ' (Exod. xxxvi.). But the workmanship of the Temple came from Phœnicia. The Hebrews were men of the field and furrow, of corn, wine, and oil. It was only when they were torn or driven from their native soil that they entered on that career of commerce and finance which forms the one art in which they have been as a race successful, and in which they seem to have found their true material function. But it would also seem as if they were kept from entering on that till they had uttered the burden of their religious testimony. To gain the world, the race had to lose its soul. It was after they had produced the great prophets that a portion of them dispersed to take the place of the Phœnicians as carriers and merchants of the ancient world. And it was only after they had exhausted themselves in the great religious birth of time, in Jesus Christ, that they ceased to be of prime importance to religious truth, and passed on to be the bankers and financiers of the modern world. But with all their wealth and commercial talent, even with all the power of thinking they showed in the Middle Ages, they have less often been original, either in thought or art. Adaptation has been their forte. No people can so adapt themselves to another people in whose midst they live. As thinkers they have chiefly shown a rare power of adapting and distributing the thought of others. The brilliant exception is Spinoza. With wealth also they have developed a fine appreciation of Art. But as artists, if we except one or two musicians—of whom I can recall at the moment only the contested Mendelssohn—they have more title to be remembered as interpreters or patrons of the masters than as masters themselves. They are great actors, but not great dramatists.

But if they have not given the world art, they have left it something far more precious. They have left it that new creative life of the soul which makes art possible. They produced that which produced Art. We have seen how close is the bond between Religion and Art, that Religion is historically the precursor of Art, or the soil from which it springs. And we have seen that the quality of the art depends on the quality of the religion. He, therefore, who by a new creation gives us an eternal faith, also opens infinite possibilities to the creation in Art. He need not be an artist who does Art its greatest service. If he supply life with heavenly love, courage, hope, and inspiration, the artist will duly arise to give to such thoughts and feelings colour and form.

One hears complaints sometimes that the Jesus even of the Transfiguration and the Resurrection had few affinities with the imaginative life, and offers few attractions to the men of intellect. And the dissatisfied virtuoso turns from the character which gathers up the spirit of Israel, and, casting longing eyes to the future, waits and hopes for the coming of one with the spirit of Jesus, the intellect of Newton, and the imagination of a Milton or a Shakespeare, all harmoniously combined. Of course, we may speculate on fantastic possibilities; but such paragons are not the method of moral and spiritual operation, so far as we can historically see. Neither science nor art craves to gather round a personal ideal, but faith does. Faith has no meaning apart from personality. And he who exalts the soul by becoming its real presence and final ideal, also exalts Art as a consequence, and prepares science. He who purifies Religion, purifies the spirit that conditions both Science and Art. He who brings God to men, and seats Him in their fearless hearts—it is he that quickens the best human powers and draws forth the best human possibility. He who creates man anew, quickens every creative power in man. A great art can only return with a great and unified faith. Make men spiritually, finally free, and the thinker and the artist will not fail from out the land. Take care of the soul, and the thought, the imagination, the skill will take care of themselves. That is now true, in the mingled influences of Aryan and Semite in Christ, which for the Semite alone was not true. The beauty of holiness will often crave, and freely find, in the beauty of Nature and Art the expression of its divine delight.

The Hebrew had the soul, but lacked the organ, the Indo-European had the organ, but was lacking in the soul. When Christ placed the soul in the eternal and final command of the world, He gave it control of the organ, and inspired imagination and skill with a new moral and spiritual life. He wedded Jew and Gentile. And the artistic as well as the philosophical history of Christendom shows the fruit of the union. Greek thought takes a Christian inspiration, Greek art receives a Christian fulness of love and soul. Hebrew spirituality receives a new flexibility, and Hebrew faith a new element of humanity and charm.

The long future of Art depends on the answer to two questions. Is Religion to die or to revive? And, Is Christ exhausted as an historic force? And these two questions are one.

IV

CHRISTIAN ART IN ITS GENERAL FEATURES

CHRISTIANITY introduced the world to a new idea on the one hand, and to a new passion on the other —and within both to a new power. The new idea was the idea of the true Infinite. The new passion was the passion of that Infinite as Love. And the new power was the power of the Holy Ghost and the Eternal life.

The lost soul was brought into an indestructible relation to the infinite, holy Love. It was both awed and stirred at the discovery that it had eternal relations and an infinite destiny. We cannot exaggerate the vast change which passed over the human spirit when it awoke to feel itself beyond the limitations of the ancient, pagan, and deliquescent world. It may, with truth, be said that all the progress of modern Europe is due to this idea of the possibility for the soul, through the grace of an infinite God, of a holy progress and destiny which were also infinite. Life received a horizon in the place of a boundary. It got impulse where it had before met only with rebuff. It felt a new right of property in this world because it had received the next in fee. There was a new power immanent in the sphere of the seen, supplied by faith's assurance of the infinite resources of the hoped-for and unseen.

This infinity which men were taught to take home to their trust was not a mathematical infinity of extension, nor a dynamical infinity of energy. It was neither the infinite of space, nor the infinite of force. It was the Infinite of spiritual thought, passion, and purpose, in a word, of personality, raised to heavenly quality, divine intensity, and universal scope. It was the infinitude of holy, redeeming Love. The awful load which was felt to hang over life, and which might at any moment drop, was swept away. Fate, with its inscrutable, and therefore incalculable, action, gave way to the trust of a God who was known to be holy Love, who was morally calculable, who might be eternally relied on to act without caprice, in the steady wisdom of His changeless nature and His redeeming will, and who could be absolutely trusted with the sinful soul, with the longing heart, with the lost and loved—with all that Life held or promised of good and dear. Men could now love boldly. There was new security given, so to speak, for the investment of the heart's capital in Life. The tenants of the world were no more at the mercy of a dubious, capricious, or selfish owner. If I may continue the image, they would be at last compensated for whatever they put on the soil or into it, when it came to leaving it. The unexhausted improvements which they left in their holding of Life would return to them again after many days. Their labour was not in vain in the

Lord. The mobility and uncertainty of paganism passed away. In importing interest, colour, and beauty into life, men came to feel they were painting in view of Eternity. For was not the Eternal Love like a red, red rose, as Dante imaged heaven? Were we not the children of One who, in perfect justice and perfect love of men, was working world without end? And those of them who rose above considerations of mere justice, enhanced life's colour and content by the ardour of the devotion with which they repaid in love that infinite Love which had made them sons of God. So that while the new sense of Infinity expanded the volume of life, raised its possibilities, and reared from the soil of faith the passion for progress in the soul, the new revelation of love, and justice, increased the colour, warmth, intensity, and variety of life, and brought to fruit in a genial air those germs of longing which the idea of Infinity had quickened into life. The divine Infinity, made historic in Christ's Incarnation, and actual in His Resurrection, expanded life, as the divine Love enriched it, without bound.

From such an impulse the greatest psychological results must sooner or later flow. If the Lord was risen, men could no more live at a poor dying rate. The new feeling of triumph and security was sure to take outward shape in powerful ways. And it would have been very strange if one of these had not been the way of Art. Love does not ignore beauty, but spiritualises it. Love is spiritual beauty, Love in mastery is spiritual power, and its influx into the world could not but issue again in a joyful birth as Art. And it was Art of a new and special kind. The classic art was not, indeed, utterly disjoined from love, but the difference between it and Christian art begins to appear when we ask what it was that was loved. The Greek loved Nature, and especially human nature: the object of Christian love, on the other hand, was not natural, but supernatural. It was spent on a spiritual object, the same in kind as the soul that loved. The Greek loved beneath him, the Christian above him. The Christian loved above his station. He loved at once his equal, whom he *could* love, and his superior, whom he had *no right* to love, the God Man, the human God, whose grace offered Himself to love. He loved a spirit, a person, like himself, not a thing; but it was a divine and holy Spirit, in whom existed complete all the perfections which his guilt had flouted, and his salvation could but share. This love, therefore, was an entirely inward matter. It could easily dispense with an outward expression. The art which bodied it forth was but an appanage, a servant, a voice. The Greek's love, on the contrary, being the love of an external thing, was not thus independent and self-sufficing. The expression of it was much less indispensable, more of its essence. The art, as I have already said, became the religion, and the religion the art. They rose and they fell together at the last. Christianity, on the other hand, has outlived several developments of Art, as it outlives many forms of society; and it is

CHRISTIAN ART

independent of them all. It is supernational in Art as in Grace. And this is further to be noticed, that even where Christian art ceases to be intensely spiritual, it does not become merely naturalistic. Between pure spirituality, or the love of the Divine Spirit, and pure naturalism, or the love of the obvious beauty, there is Humanity, the love of the dear, near human heart and soul. Even when Art drops from the pure spiritual region of a Fra Angelico, it does not become a pure paganism, or worship of natural and outward form; but still, if it deserve a Christian name at all, or the epithet great, it is concerned with the affections of the human heart, and bestows its sympathy on the idylls or the tragedies of a human soul. Art, if it be noble, must forget itself; and Christian art, if it do not lose itself in the Divine Spirit, is yet too spiritual to bestow its entire affection on mere Nature. It abandons itself to a sympathy with human joy, love, sorrow, hope, or death, which is soothing where it is not sublime. If it love not the Infinite Spirit, it loves a finite spirit:

> But yet a spirit still, and bright
> With something of angelic light.[1]

It does not worship in the world of the seen, the physical, the formal, and sculpturesque. Man's soul, or his heart, not his body, is its theme. The Greek sculptor worshipped Nature as human. The Christian artist has a far deeper note, for he loves human nature; and he develops a new realism out of the deeper and more spiritual affection.

[1] Wordsworth: "She was a phantom of delight."

You will quote, perhaps, as hardly bearing out what I have just said, the art movement known as Pre-Raphaelitism; and you point to the tendency, not only to paint landscape (which might be charged with human passion or sentiment), but to depict with extreme accuracy of form and colour little 'bits' of Nature—nooks of wild country, patches of open sea, reaches of tossed or tranquil cloud, descending even to flowers, fruit, leaves, fragments of a single plant or scene. Is that not pure naturalism? Surely no. What is it that has moved men with the artistic gift to spend their lives and talents on such work, if it be not remotely the Christian conviction, in them or their society, that, in a far closer sense than the Psalmist meant it, the earth is the Lord's, and the fulness thereof, and that the wealth of Nature's beauty is but the reflection of the immanent beauty of the Infinite Spirit, who moves and lives and has His being in it all? I do not say this thought is always, or even generally, present in such an artist's mind, but surely, after Holman Hunt's writing, we may say it underlies the strength of the movement. And besides, what constitutes even a Pre-Raphaelite picture, what makes it more than photographic *genre*, is something beyond mere accuracy of representation. It is something that makes the artist different, his feeling, his insight, his soul.

And this leads me to ask here, as I did in respect of Hellenic and Hebrew art, What is the relation between the human spirit and outward nature which makes Christian art? I have spoken of the relation between the soul and God. What is that between the soul and Nature ? In Indian art we found the vastness of Nature pressing on the mind, and crushing it into deformity or helplessness. In the art of Egypt we found mind emerging like the head of the Sphinx from the body of the beast, and striving to assert for itself an independent, or at least an equal, place. In Greece it had gained that place. We found that mind and Nature there were peers, acting and interacting in full and blithe harmony, each adequate to the other, and each happy. We had, in consequence, an art limited, indeed, but perfect, and a balance which the world will probably never see again. In Israel we started from the opposite pole. We had to do with another and quite different branch of our race. We found, instead of matter dominating and crushing the soul, the moral soul mastering and crushing matter. So impressive, so imperious, was the spirituality, that it might be said often to domineer rather than to rule. Natural beauty was ignored or pushed aside. Its voice was silenced beside the awful presence of the divine Soul, and the huge imperative of His holy name; and the faculties which link man with Nature were stunted and discouraged, that the one channel of communication upwards with God might be kept clear. Nature was not, indeed, severed from God, but she was regarded rather as the slave than the child, or even the servant, of the Almighty. She was His creature, and expressed His power. She did not reflect His character, but was the agent of His power. 'When I consider the heavens,' says the Psalm, 'I am amazed at thy power, O God, and I am forced to marvel that Thou regardest man at all.' Whereas the Christian astronomer,[1] as he traced the structure of the heavens, gloried not alone in the sense of divine power, but in the knowledge of divine thought. 'I think God's thoughts after Him,' he said. One sentence, which I quoted,[2] contains the whole matter: 'Nature with this people was undeified, but not yet understood.' The witness it bore to its Creator was like the rude and early witness of the Spirit in the first babbling Christian communities. It was confused, inordinate, inarticulate, unintelligible. Nature here was not God; it only bore witness of God. And its gift of tongue was thick and broken, like the utterance of a God-intoxicated soul.

The Christian mind is the reconciliation of Jew and Greek. A stage has been reached, by help of the Jew, beyond the Greek balance of body and soul, and, by the help of the Greek, beyond speechless awe. Mind has exactly reversed its place in India, and has now been lifted to look down on the matter which once bruised it with its heel. But to look down only as the Jew did. This transcendence of matter by soul, is it no more than the Jew instinctively realised, and received naïvely as a gift from heaven? No, it is not the same. It is something richer, fuller, more precious in every way. It is not transcendence, and it is not immanence. It is the immanence of the transcendent. We do not singly have the benefit of God's tran-

[1] Kepler. [2] Hegel: see pp. 61, 62.

scendence of the world; we share it and its immanence.

There are men and women whose faith from their early years is simple, ready, and sure. They are not the victims of a deadly struggle. It is not theirs to clear a path with spiritual agony from darkness into light, and rise from despair into faith and hope. But that is the heavy destiny of many another, who only comes to the simplicity of trust in his later years, and only gains the peace of confident love after he has been exercised and strengthened by the searching conflict of many a spiritual fight. Is that late-won faith just the same as the early trust which seemed to come into life with the temperament, as a natural endowment and personal gift? Is the faith of the twice-born worth no more than that of the once-born? Surely no. He who has fought his way to light has a grasp and sinew denied to the other's gentle trust, and a power to lift others to his side. He knows the ground he has covered with armed vigilance as the cheery traveller does not. He has a power of sympathy with other serious wayfarers which is absent in those to whom the burden was light. And to the faith of the warrior a whole world of deep significance and rich association lies open, where the more childlike mood feels but a vague spiritual presence and a dim sense of voiceless, balmy breath.

Such, in a way, is the difference between the native, though serious, spirituality of Israel and the hard-won, penetrating spirituality reached at last by the Western Christian mind in a wider world. I pointed out, in dealing with Hebrew religion, that this race had not the eye which perceives the finer shades of natural beauty, or of moral conflict and spiritual degree. And one reason is that spirituality did not cost them so much as it involved to the Western mind. They had not gone sounding on the spirit's dim and perilous way as the Aryan family had done. They were never at home in Nature, and had never its patriotism or its pride. They had not the warrior's knowledge of the ground, that sense of the perils, or that sympathy with the varied phases of the spiritual country which grows up in those who linger, explore, and fight in it. The soul and the world were certainly regions not unknown to the Jew, and not unfelt. But to the Indo-European mind, quickened by Jewish faith, they are more than felt, they are searched and understood. The ancient Greek transfused Nature with thought and imagination, lingered upon it, and discovered in it a fine significance and a subtle law. The Jew made it but a stepping-stone to heaven, a mere pendant of God. To the Greek the world was his familiar home, to the Jew only his inn. Now, if we could join these conceptions, should we not have the Christian mind? If we marry penetrative Greek imagination to masterful Jewish spirituality, have we not that spiritual imagination which is the artistic feature of Christendom? We have soul supreme —first, the infinite Soul, and then, through Him,

CHRISTIAN ART

the finite soul of man. And we have Nature, not, indeed, as an equal, not a consort of soul, but, at the same time, not crushed, a friend and not a slave. If a servant, she was a servant so congenial, so prompt, and so plastic that she might also be a friend and dear companion, nay, a representative, and even a word charged with the soul's thought, not to speak of God's. The ground-plan of Nature was now Redemption. The sphere of Nature, which the Greek had leavened with his thought, received now a consecration from God's will and purpose, which developed new values for the heart, and inspired a thought and sympathy still more searching and subtle than Greece could infuse. It became charged in every part with the thought and love of the Infinite. It became a part of the divine Word. It was a revelation, not of the Creator's power only, but also of His character and intent. There was an organic connection set up between God and the world which the Jew would have mostly thought impious. It was not, however, a monistic connection of organic equality, but one of created dependence. Nature was not the bride, but the child. Still, it is not strange if some went so far as to regard Nature as more than a creation and a revelation, if they treated it as an incarnation or a pantheistic epiphany of God.

The Christian conception, then, differed from the Greek in that it placed soul, not on a level with Nature, but clearly and eternally above it. Yet it differed from the Jewish conception in that it interpenetrated Nature with spirit, refined the connection between them, and made the relation a far more intimate one than that of the craftsman and his handicraft. It reconciled the immanence and the eminence of God. It lifted the visible to the dignity of reflecting and witnessing the mind of the Invisible and Eternal. Both Spirit and Nature, man and the world, were thus exalted together. And though many phases of Christianity seek to enhance the one at the other's expense, yet the large and general tendency of this revelation has been otherwise. It has uplifted our thought together of the Creator and the work. It has blessed both Him that gives and that which takes. And we have here an illustration of the first principle of true progress. Raise the conception of God, and the faith in Him, and you will not only exalt the soul's power but deepen its insight into Nature. The revelation of Christianity had thus the twofold effect upon the human spirit. It exalted and expanded its characteristic powers by a release from the world, and, on the other hand, it gave it a new interest and sympathy with the world. Man by redemption became free *from* the world *for* the world. The very influence that made the soul independent of Nature gave it in the same act a power over Nature, and an understanding of it, which the Greek relation of equality did not develop. It gave it leisure from itself to sympathise. The soul *descended* on Nature like a heavenly hero, and forced from her moods of submission, works of service, and secrets of charm which she will yield only to a mastery truly sympathetic and divine.

Now these two effects of Christianity took shape in two great artistic changes.

1. First, New arts, if they did not come into existence, were thrust into the foreground.

2. And Second, The features of these new arts were impressed on all art. The new power of the soul uttered itself not only in the new departments of painting and music, but in the fresh and novel treatment of all artistic themes.

Let me take the second first.

2. Several new artistic features appear in Christian art, features which were to antique art almost or entirely unknown. There have been indicated by Hegel at least three tendencies in Christian art which are peculiarly its own, associated with the new love and its spirit of tender play.

(i) The tendency to the fantastic.
(ii) The tendency to the grotesque.
(iii) The tendency to the picturesque.

(i) The fantastic art of Christendom belongs to an early period of it. It is exemplified in what are known as arabesques. In that form of decoration you have the exuberant play of a powerful imagination, which is as yet in the childish stage, which has not become earnest, and entered on the severe study of Nature and its laws. Lines and circles move and interweave in such a way as to defy all law, but they yet retain a marvellous freedom and subdued method. There are no complete circles, there are no right angles. There is the Oriental feature of perpetual surprise. The lines, as you trace them, perpetually disappoint you, in the most interesting way. Just as you think the circle will be completed, you find it trends away into some other graceful and incalculable curve. And when you believe a right angle is inevitable, the pencil coyly swerves, and you are ingeniously cheated and skilfully mocked. This feature is not confined, however, to arabesques, but is exemplified still more strikingly in other decorations, *e.g.*, the fantastic heads and creatures which serve as spouts, brackets, corbels, or finials in the cathedrals. And its incarnation is the mediæval devil. There is a wilfulness, an elfishness, about the style which makes it attractive to a people with plenty of raw artistic force but little discipline. It charms, as the same thing in a girl might attract and amuse a strong, crude, easy man. The Oriental facility in this fantastic direction did thus charm and exercise Christian Europe in its first ages of imaginative power. Christendom, like a young barbarian, with its latent vigour of spirit, loved to sport in this free and yet graceful fashion. The fantastic element in Christian art is a result of the new power infused into the human mind by the new inspiration of Christianity. This fantasy was the second childhood of the old religions. But it was the first childhood of Christianity, its morning twilight. It testifies in the far East only to the impotence of the faith, or the senility of the race. We find it only in the later stages of classic art, and it bears witness there to the effeteness of a creed that allowed the imagination to sink, and the soul to amuse its enfeebled self with the trivialities of an art once great and strong. But it is in the infancy, not in the decay, of Christian art that it appears. And it has therefore a very different significance. The boy makes nimble play with the old man's carved staff. It speaks, not of fading power, but of the sportive power which is just coming to a consciousness of itself. It is the twilight of the dawn, not of the night. It is the exuberant expression of a new sense of the soul's mastery over Nature and natural law. It is a youthful defiance of rule, and the vehement assertion of new freedom in creation. It is a young giant's *tour de force.* Moreover, what is fantastic in ancient art confined itself to distorting natural forms. The fantastic in Christian art, on the contrary, has no exclusive connection with natural forms. It is not imitative only. It is simply the free play of a hand urged to graceful freaks by a superabundance of vitality in the spirit behind it.

(ii) We have this passing into humorous or grotesque. Very much might be said, and has been said, about Christian humour and its great divergence from the classic forms. If we except dramatic poetry, there was little humour in ancient art, and what was in poetry was of a less humane sort, and constantly tended, in the presence of growing moral corruption, to degenerate through wit into satire. The laugh was of a dry, intellectual, and incisive, rather than of a genial, sympathetic, or extravagant sort, and not infrequently it became ghastly. It certainly had pathos and no twinkle. But the humour of the Christian stage is of a loving, sympathetic, and pitiful sort; the wit does twinkle, it does not merely flash; and the laugh lies much nearer to the spring of tears than anything that antiquity can show. The hard gaiety of the old world is replaced by kindly humour in the new. If Christ never laughed, at least He taught men a new and deeper smile. There is all the Christian world of difference between the humour of Aristophanes and that of Shakespeare. Aristophanes did not love or pity Socrates in the least when he hung him up in a basket in the *Clouds*. But Shakespeare did both love and pity that 'tun of a man' whose gross life ended babbling of green fields. And again, what a difference between Juvenal and Cervantes. Indeed, the great loveless humorist of Christian times stands out as a sort of monster or anomaly, and has, like the ash-tree in the field, a wide bare space round him, where his fellow-men and fellow-geniuses do not grow, and do not love to come.

The grotesque ensues when the humour is either less earnest or more extravagant, and merely sportive. But it is never totally devoid of some latent spiritual significance. You have obvious examples of it in those ridiculous figures which are frequently to be seen projecting from cathedral or abbey walls, representations, not fantastic merely like elaborate scrolls or impossible griffins, but purely ludicrous, such as a pig playing the bagpipes, or a monk groaning and twisting his face under the weight of a statue in a niche, or pulling his mouth out with his fingers towards his ears, with countless objects of a similar kind. Often the intention is clearly satire. You find it also in those pictures so common in the Middle Ages called the Dance of Death. And there is a memorable specimen of it in Orcagna's picture, 'The Triumph of Death,' where the great ones of the world are placed in front of three decaying bodies, and one of the princes is holding his nose. I may also mention the grim humour of Albert Dürer, and the very quaint tender poems in the 'Wunderhorn.' I have seen abroad a mediæval bas-relief of the Nativity (I think at Huy), where a cow is licking the Baby's face.

Now all this is utterly foreign to classic art, and much of it is foreign to the art and taste of our own day. How is it to be explained? It is of priceless historical importance, whatever judgment be passed on it in the interest of ideal art. It is priceless, I say, as an historical indication of the religious mind of the age. It sprang from three sources.

(*a*) It had its origin, first and generally, where the fantastic element in early Christian art had its source—in the new power and freedom which had been infused into the human spirit, and the consequent new disposition to revel, free of the restraints of taste and law, for the fun of the thing, in that which is simply incongruous and surprising.

(*b*) It arose, second and more particularly, from

the new sense of sympathy and kindness which men experienced in feeling themselves to be redeemed. They were no more dogged by a mysterious Fate or pursued by avenging furies. They were saved and surrounded by an omnipresent love. They recovered some of the lightness of the olden time, though it was gaiety with a chastened note. They had passed through the knowledge of sin before they reached their freedom. This chastened the joy in its tone, and invested it with certain associations of tenderness and sadness. But it had also a contrary effect on the form of the mirth as distinct from its tone. The rebound of joy in the feeling of escape from sin was so violent that it took the almost boisterous expression. The more absurd the grotesquery, the more expressive it would be of the violent jubilance of their naïve natures. They had the passions of men with the intelligence of children in that strange Middle Age. And their mirth was stirred by devices which, if they have a suggestion of manly sadness in their tone, have yet the expression of a boyish extravagance in their form.

(c) But it arose thirdly from the new sense of the greatness of God, life, and the soul. Such humour is one of the modes in which man views the huge disparity between the finite world and the infinite beyond. In some moods this is a solemn reflection, or it leads to the classic irony which saw all things in the idea, and yet all things as nothing in the idea. In certain other states it finds expression and relief in laughter. The world's

CHRISTIAN ART

pettiness at one moment irritates us, and at another, measured against the world's vast and blessed issues, it moves us to a smile, now tender only, now tender and grim (as in Carlyle). United in spirit ourselves with the Infinite and Eternal, we see the trivialities of life as Gulliver watched the Lilliputians climbing over his boots. Now the great outburst of humour in Art in the Middle Age is due ultimately, but not consciously, to the importation into all the world's affairs of the new feeling of the Infinite. It could not happen in the first years of Christianity, for then the Infinite was too near and solemnising a presence. The soul was absorbed and engaged with God. But when the newness of the divine Presence was removed without taking away the security, and the dazzled eyes returned to the light and objects of common earth, then the disparity, the contrast, began to be felt; and it was joined with a great pity; and then there stole over the face of Europe the dawn of that tender and sympathetic smile which wreathed the lips of Shakespeare, reigned on Jean Paul's brow, and sweetened the incisive veracity of George Eliot and Carlyle. This humour could not emerge in ancient Greece, for there the horizon of life was too limited, and Destiny was not that true and placable Infinite which makes a background for the laughter that is in little things. To laugh divinely you must project the finite upon an infinite grace. The grotesque art of the Middle Ages, and the sweeter, deeper humour of a later time, stand out upon a background of the merciful and gracious eternity assured by the revelation of Christ.

(iii) The third feature which distinguished Christian art is the feature of the picturesque. This, of course, recalls the fact that painting rose to a new place as an art, but it implies more. Just as sculpture was the art which set the pitch for all other art in Greece, so, we may say, painting gives the note for all the arts in Christianity. Christian art is everywhere picturesque rather than statuesque. It is deep, not superficial. It utters a soul, it does not simply present a form. It embodies action rather in passion than in calm, and action as an expression of character and individuality. Sculpture, we saw, cares rather to express a noble type of ideal beauty than an engaging peculiarity of individual character. Portraiture, therefore, is not of much account. In Christendom, on the other hand, it has a high, if not the highest, place in pictorial art. Grouping or composition, moreover, is a feature, if not peculiar to Christian art, at any rate distinctive of it, and grouping is a pictorial, not a statuesque effect. Sculpture, again, avoided all representation of extreme passion or tumult of soul. The Laocoon is more prized in modern times than it was in its ancient world. But Christian art would be non-existent without passion and its picturesque resources and effects.

Christian art, we may say then, is picturesque. And this means more, as I say, than the mere fact that landscape painting is a product of the

Christian age. It implies that the methods of painting are such as have a close affinity with the principles of Christian spirituality, freedom, infinitude, and truth. Colour is a more spiritual agent than form. ' Colour,' says Ruskin, ' is the spiritual power of art.' Colour, we might say, is the religion, and form the theology, of art. Light, which gives colour its value, is more than a symbol; it may be a very part of the light which lighteth every man, part of the radiance of reason and the power of the Spirit. And the representations of painting work by an illusion which transcends sense and appeals to an intellectual process behind the seeing of the eye. A figure carved in stone appeals but to the sense for its realisation as a figure. But a figure painted to look as if it stood out involves a mental process; part of which is a tacit protest against trusting to sense; for sense would tell us that it is a mere flat surface that we see, and not a rounded image at all. Painting, therefore, not only suffers, but demands the preponderance of the inward over the outward, of the spirit over the body of sense. Its tendency is, like the natural blue of heaven and of night, to deepen on our gaze, and cast us onward into an infinity of meaning, of passion, of character, of beauty. It does not, like sculpture, rivet our gaze on perfection of form and material finality, apart from the soul behind. Spirituality, infinity, and passion find their way to utterance through the pictorial in Art as they do not through anything in the ancient world. Let me say that

I am not here putting the art of painting above poetry or music. I am not now speaking of this or that art. I mean a particular element in all art, inadequately named the picturesque, the element which, to convey Art's revelation, employs the deep significance of colour and composition rather than the significance of form and figure. 'There is no outline in Nature,' says a modern painter. It is the melting shades of colour, and the melting contours of landscape, whether in poetry or painting, that best suit with those suggestions of the Infinite which abhor the sharpness of definition and transcend the limitation of form.

That the Impressionists have carried this to an extreme does not destroy its truth. And, moreover, in the composition or grouping of pictorial art, whether in painting a scene, or composing a poem, or a sonata—it is there you find that creative subjection and sacrifice of the part to the sum, of the individual to the whole, which is such a feature of Christian ethics and Christian creed. It is thus that we see the pageantry of history, not merely passing away, but taken up into the spiritual world:

> These our actors,
> As I foretold you, were all spirits, and
> Are melted into air, into thin air;
> And, like the baseless fabric of this vision,
> The cloud-capt towers, the gorgeous palaces,
> The solemn temples, the great globe itself,
> Yea, all which it inherit, shall dissolve;

> And like this insubstantial pageant faded,
> Leave not a rack behind. We are such stuff
> As dreams are made on, and our little life
> Is rounded with a sleep.[1]

There, too, you find that pervasion of the most various whole by a supreme thought or passion which is the Christian view of the universe and of human fate. It is in the pictorial treatment of things that we find artistic echo of the reconciliation between the finite and the Infinite, the form and the soul, the body and the spirit. And it is there, in the element of colour, that we find fit expression of that warm passion and varied emotion which the passionate love of God has evoked in men towards each other and towards Himself. We see, in

> Celestial rosy red, love's proper hue.

And it is in the resources of colour alone that we find utterance for that melting desire, that *nuance* of yearning, with which the pathetic helplessness of mobile and manifold man craves for the infinite fulness of God. It is the melting, flowing, significance of conjoined line, colour, and arrangement that fitly bodies forth that high travail of the finite to be taken up continually into the Infinite, of the carnal to become spiritualised, of the creature to be manifested as a son of Eternal God.

[1] The Tempest, iv, i.

V

PAINTING—I

I HAVE said that of all the plastic arts painting is the most Christian. And I meant it specially in this sense. Not that the art of painting is in itself a more distinctly Christian product than, say, music, for much might be said for music as the specially Christian art. But I meant this, that the type of art introduced by painting, and the emotions and thoughts expressed by it and its methods, are, when compared with either sculpture or architecture, distinctively Christian and spiritual. Leaving music, therefore, out of account for the present, we may say that painting is the Christian art among the arts that are representative.

Historically, at any rate, painting is a product of the Christian age. The ancients had fine and famous paintings, as I have already owned, but the art did not express, fascinate, and absorb ancient genius as it has done that of the moderns under Christianity. It seems to follow from this that there must be some congruity and even affinity between the spirit and teaching of Christianity, on the one hand, and the genius, methods, and materials of this art on the other. In this lecture I will ask what this ideal affinity is, and I will leave to another occasion what I have to say about the actual and historical connection. I hope at least, here as elsewhere, to suggest the presumption, if not to impress the conviction, that there is a most real and deep connection between the spiritual condition, or the intellectual belief, of an age and the artistic products of it, and that the latter is, more or less, the reflection of the former.

We might begin by asking what was the fresh preoccupation of religious thought in the ages in which painting rose and reached its height. We should be careful lest we fall victims to the error that theology produces, or ever did produce, Art. It does no such thing. If it did it would be easier to trace the connection, and clearer than I can hope to make it. But the same principles in the nature of Christianity which in one direction produced theology took shape in another, but parallel, direction as art. Now the ruling idea when Christian art arose in the Middle Ages was the idea of Reconciliation, especially as connected with the theory and discipline of penance. That was the idea which was at the heart of all the religious thought of the period. The origins of painting nearly coincided with the beginnings of serious thought on the method and the nature of the Atonement. The date of Anselm, the first real thinker on Reconciliation, is, roundly, 1100 A.D. The contemporary art of architecture, in its Gothic style, went as far as such an art could go in expressing these religious ideas; and then painting took the torch from the hands of the great builders, and began its career as great art in the person of Giotto, whose date is roughly 1300 A.D. Speculation is all this time busied with great energy on the questions which Anselm had roused.

Now, as to the meaning of the word Reconciliation. The idea has two stages. There is the stage of mutual toleration, and there is the stage of mutual understanding; the stage of mere intercourse, and that of sympathy or communion. May I use a scientific metaphor? There is the mechanical mixture as of two kinds of grain, and there is the chemical mixture of two kinds of fluid, or, still more intimately, two substances with a chemical affinity for each other. So a man may be reconciled to another man and henceforth they go through life transacting business together, and accepting the usual routine of social life, with an understanding good enough for the purposes of ordinary comfort, that bygones shall be bygones. But a real reconciliation means more than that. Bygones are actually explained and adjusted, they are not merely avoided or forgotten. Respect is superseded by love. Intercourse passes into a deeper sympathy. The falling out of faithful friends is the renewing of love. And there is a communion of spirit with spirit, and heart with heart, which binds the two parties in a bond more deep, lasting, and sacred than anything which held them before. In the previous case the two come to understand each other's ways. In the latter they come to understand each other's heart and thought.

Now with this in mind, at the risk of wearying

PAINTING

you, but for the sake of clearness, let me again hurry you over these steps of development which we have seen the mind of man to undergo. This time we will look at them in the light of this idea of Reconciliation. We found the man confronted by two vastly greater powers, physical Nature and the Almighty. Nature, we found, confronted the Indo-European family. Spirit we found pressing upon the Semitic family. We began with one extremity of the Indo-European race in India, and we found there the human spirit crushed and distorted under the vastness of Nature. There was no reconciliation. The two forces were in antagonism, and the one was the tyrant of the other. We passed through Egypt and saw the spirit beginning to lift its head and claim some equality with Nature. And then we reached the other extremity of the Aryan family, Greece, to find at last spirit and nature in one accord, of one mind, dwelling together in entire amity, each satisfied with the other, each adequate to the other on the plane they had reached. We found Nature interpenetrated by the human mind, and able to be a complete and satisfying expression of its nature. Here, then, you have Reconcilement of a very intimate sort. Man and Nature are at one, with a mutual adaptation which the Greek statue so exquisitely bodies forth.

But the end was not yet. There was a higher plane with a new harmony. There were capabilities in the human soul still to be developed, which should reduce classic Nature to the old inadequacy, and bring that romantic yearning and aspiration into art which reflects the travail of creation for the manifestation of the sons of God.

In the other, the Semitic, family, it is not Nature which confronts man, it is God. That is, spirit in man faces, not matter, but Spirit in God. But at first we found the divine Spirit lying on the human with a load like the load of Nature upon the Indian. We found the activities of the Semitic soul crushed, and the edge of his sensibility blunted, by the pressure upon his reverence of this omnipotent Spirit. In the Jews, as the foremost family of the Semitic race, we found the pressure lightened. We found sympathy entering into the relations of man and God. Their art, their lyric poetry especially, showed this. We found a degree of reconciliation reached between God and man which has its chief expression in moral forgiveness, but which has not yet attained to true spiritual communion and entire fusion of sympathy. The servant knew not what his Lord did. The union is still (if I may use the image without impropriety) somewhat mechanical, not chemical; it is legal rather than spiritual. Justification has not yet passed into true reconciliation, into that sanctification which possesses at once communion with God and insight into the nature of those holy conditions on which it rests. This completeness of reconciliation, it was the work of Christianity to effect. By Christianity we have spirit perfectly reconciled with spirit, and a relation set up between God and man parallel to that which on the lower level was established between man and Nature in Greece. Parallel, but not identical; much higher. For the Greek idea was harmony, in the sense of symmetry and proportion of parts, while the Christian was that of atonement, or the reconciliation of persons. The one was æsthetic, the other moral. And the pagan side of even Christian art clung to the Greek idea. But it was at least the faith of the ages which bred the great painters that, as the artistic spirit of Phidias was infused into the marble, and fully incarnated there, so the holy Spirit of God was infused into the human soul of Christ and incarnated there. The great difference, of course, was that in the Greek case we have personality saturating matter, in the Christian a person inspiring a person. The reconciliation between the divine Spirit and humanity was such that the one became the adequate, if not the total, utterance of the other. You see, then, how the two races combine and contribute in Christianity. The Semites supply the two parties and declare them to be not soul and Nature, but soul and soul. They supply the elements, the quantities, so to speak, as moral quantities on each side, and declare that reconciliation must be by redemption. The Indo-Europeans, the Greeks, supply the idea of their relationship, the idea of complete intimacy and spiritual fusion, the idea of entire reconciliation by the way of incarnation. I have already mentioned the very important fact that incarnation is not a Hebrew idea, but a Greek or Indian one; the Hebrew idea is redemption. The Greek relation of the two Hebraic factors becomes an actual, historic, experimental fact in Christianity. And we have an Incarnation which operates as a reconciliation through redemption.

Now, it is the joint idea of incarnation and reconcilement which is at the root of Christian art, and especially painting. But the type of classical art could not be an adequate vehicle for this Christian idea and spirit. It is only to a limited degree that architecture can express this spirit; and we shall see that a new style of architecture had to be invented for the special object of expressing as much of it as it did. Architecture, speaking as it does mostly in the language of inorganic nature, could not express fully a faith centring round a human being. And sculpture, the typical Greek art, could not express the Christian idea either. For its ideal is beauty of form, and it expresses, not the incarnation of the divine Spirit in the human soul, but only of the human soul in the human body. The type of art required was one which should express more than Greek sculpture, that entire inwardness and spirituality, yet that intense and deep passion, that independence of the material, and yet that intense interest in it, which both mark the Christian idea. Art was not itself to be the incarnation, as was the case in Greece; it was only to bear witness of an incarnation foregone. It was to be a reflection of the spiritual light at a bright angle into the heaven from which it came. The sphere of incarnation was moved higher, beyond

Nature, beyond the body, into the region of the spirit itself, and reflection was all that was left to Art with its material organ and deified body. Christianity was God incarnate in human nature, and not in a human body chiefly. That fact makes a great difference in the relations between Religion and Art. It is pagan art, whether in Michel Angelo or Rubens, which deifies the creature, heroises the bodily form, makes the saints courtly and superior persons, the apostles stately, or even gigantic, lords of the superman rather than of the God Man. And it is Christian art which goes to the realism of human nature, as Rembrandt did, and finds the divine most present in the form of servants, poor and laden, where humanity has little but its human nature, and yet that can be divine—without façades, feasts, processions, or poses of ambitious sort. Christian art is the art of the heart and the soul with all its chiaroscuro, rather than of mere healthiness and the mere natural competent tasteful man. And its genius can do more with loving the rude than with lighting the nude.

You may see, perhaps, that it is only from a very intimate reconciliation of the soul with its high object that great art can proceed. The art of Greece sprang out of the intimate harmony set up between man and Nature, soul and body; the art of Christianity from the intimate sympathy and close understanding set up between man and God, soul and soul. Greek art is the reconciliation of spirit and matter; Christian art the recon.

ciliation of spirit and spirit, and especially by way of the conscience, by the moral or the holy Spirit. The nations which do not realise any, or any great, intimacy of such Reconciliation have either no art, or a very imperfect type of it, nothing worth the name of great Art. Hence the artistic poverty of the Jew and the Hindoo.

Christianity, then, repaired the discord of the world in terms, not of matter, but of spirit, not of charm, but of conscience, not of mere process, but of moral action. It was inward, spiritual, and free. The art, therefore, which would reflect it should tend to this inwardness, this spirituality, this moral freedom. It should in its methods direct our attention away from material things, and be itself, as it were, passing away into the spiritual world. It must use, as its organ or medium, a form of matter so fine as to be just on the borderland where sense ceases and soul begins. A solid substance like marble does not satisfy this condition. An ethereal substance like light or colour does; sculpture therefore is not spiritual, painting is.

In this direction there is a remarkable progress shown by the arts in their historical succession. The arts more recently developed make use of a more refined and rarefied medium than those first developed. And as a consequence they become capable of expressing with greater and greater delicacy fine shades of emotion and perception. What is the historical order of the arts? It is sculpture, architecture, painting, music, and, in a certain sense, poetry. (For the poetry of Christian Europe is greater than anything in antiquity.) Now is that not also their order if you arrange them according to the tenuity of their medium? Thus. The medium or material of sculpture is marble, and the effect of that art is quite inseparable from the quality of mass, or at least palpability, in the material. Its grace is divine, but not unearthly. It can repose in Nature, and have on earth an abiding place. The material in architecture is also stone, but it is stone treated, as we shall see in Gothic, so as to throw down the massive effect, and throw up the effect of extreme grace and vanishing lightness. It is stone made spiritual and musical—' a symphony in stone.' It is unearthly. It is in flight, and not in repose. On earth it has no abiding. These two arts, however, are more nearly on the same footing in this respect than either of them is when compared with painting. Here you have the material element extremely rarefied. You are made quite independent of the effect of mass in the material, and you are obliged to do everything with much more subtle and slender means—with light, and colour, and a flat surface. Pass onward to music, and what do you find? You find the material element almost erased. You find space and mass dispensed with. You are made dependent on time and tone alone. And whereas, in appreciating the effects of painting, you have to call at least two senses into play—the sense of sight, and the muscular sense (or three with the sense of touch)—in the case of music you have but the one sense, that of hearing. So that if a man were born with only a retina, without power to move his eye or his limbs, he would not be able to enjoy painting; whereas a man born with only the auditory nerve active, with the sense of hearing alone, might be able to enjoy music. And then, when we come to poetry, it is true it is not the last of the arts to be developed. It is rather true that it has gone on alongside of the other arts. But its greatest and widest effects have been in the modern, Christian, and spiritual time. Well, what do we find there? Why, no material medium at all. Space and time both abolished, the images and forms existing only in the imagination of the poet and his reader or hearer. But, you say, there is the print, or the voice, things of space or of time. Yes, but these are not the material or medium of poetry in the sense in which marble is the material of sculpture, or colour of painting. The print or the voice in this case is not part of the art. The print may be very bad and the art first-rate, as in a shilling Shakespeare. The print here is only the coffer in which the work of art is kept, the rude ark in which is deposited the eternal fertility of the rod that buds green, the tablets of beauty's eternal law and the heavenly manna of poetic passion or thought. The print is to the poetic art what the pedestal is to the statue or the canvas to the picture. And the voice need not be there at all. It is an entirely spiritual medium that the poet uses to set forth and convey his spirit. It is imaginative thought, emotion, and action by which he utters soul. Whereas in the other arts the thoughts and the emotions themselves, by which we reach the artist's soul behind, have to be conveyed by the intervention of a material means more or less refined.

It is, to say the least, striking to find this progressive attenuation of the material going side by side with the growing delicacy, refinement, and spirituality of human nature itself; and to note that, whenever the soul would take a new flight of sacrifice and elevation, the Lord, as it were, provides the appropriate material and channel for the burnt-offering.

Let us now go a little into detail; and let us ask this question. If Christianity be, as it has been described, so spiritual, so inward, so little sensuous, and yet so charged with intense love, pity, and interest towards the outer world; so penetrating, mobile, and pliant, and yet rooted in a confident calm; so manifold, yet so much one, so possessed of all things, yet so independent of all things, so rich and yet so poor, so absorbent and yet so renunciatory; if Christianity be so, in what respects does its art, and especially its painting, reflect these features? In what way does it reflect the reconciliation of these contradictions which is effected in the spiritual region by Christianity? Do not forget that the great and precious thing is the Reconciliation as an experienced reality—the possession by a human being of a spirit of piety and faith in which these paradoxes lie 'quiet, happy, and suppressed '—a spiritual condition possible only when the soul is taken up into God and finds its rest and completion there. It is a life hidden with Christ in God, such a life as is typified by the constant symbol in Catholic art of the Virgin and Child. If you could have asked any of the greatest Madonna painters which was the most precious thing—the soul of the Virgin, filled and pacified as they believed it to have been, or the soul of the artist who strove with his brush to reflect the uplifted and becalmed spirit of the divine Mother, or the work of art itself, which came from his hand— what would they have said ? They would not have been so great if they could have given any answer but this. Of all these precious and divine things the most precious, and most divine and blessed, is the soul of her whose sense of self and separate life was lost in worship of her Child and God. Or it was the soul of the divine Child and Redeemer in whom the Mother already worships God. But, wherever realised, this reconcilement of the world's contradictions by faith in a reconciliation in God, complete, sufficing, and final, is the pearl of great price, the one thing needful to the soul. It is not needful that we should see all things reconciled if we but wholly trust One who does. It is that which Art at its highest only partially reflects, and it can only partially reflect it to the end. For which reason the perfectness of Greek art is to Christian art for ever impossible.

Now let us turn to the features in painting

PAINTING

which, whether in Raphael or Rembrandt, enable it fitly to reflect, though not adequately to express, the Christian soul, in its inwardness, its spirituality, its faith, its love, its cross crowned with resurrection, its reconciliation of all things, and its triumph in conclusive bliss and the serene result of all.

1. There is the feature already referred to of the attenuated material used, as compared with sculpture. This gives the art a new power to express the delicacy of spiritual processes, and reach recesses of the soul which the marble cannot reach. And the attenuation referred to has two aspects.

(*a*) In regard to the dimensions of space. The statue stands out a real thing, a mass, with all the three dimensions of length, breadth, and thickness. That of itself increases the distance between the statue and the soul. For spirit is not a thing of dimensions at all. An emotion or a thought is not measurable by inches. Whatever, therefore, decreases the material extension of the work of art brings it so far nearer as an expression of the spirit. Now, in painting, the three dimensions are done away with. Instead of mass we have only a flat surface to deal with. That of itself is a great step in the dematerialising of the art.

(*b*) But further, we have this attenuation also in the nature of the agent employed. Instead of marble we have light, shade, and colour. Without going into niceties about the essence of light, in so far as it is material it is the vibration of matter of a very fine and imponderable sort. Its base is the ether which permeates all matter, and may fill all space, which is the transition between matter and spirit, and where sense slips into soul, and none can seize the moment of change. This surely places in the power of painting a subtle means for dealing with inward and spiritual facts, and bringing them to outward and visible sign. And as this substance has no weight, it is not affected by gravitation, and seems to be thrown above the earth by the weight of denser matter,—it becomes a fit index of the heavenward movement of the Christian soul. It is ideal, pervasive, piercing, and bathing all things. Its affinity is with the inward light, the reason, the spirit; and it is the outward semblance of that uncreated word which pierceth to the dividing asunder of the joints and marrow, and is a discerner of the thoughts and intents of the heart. Now this is the very power which painting has so conspicuously above sculpture, the power of finding and uttering deep and subtle shades of character and moods of feeling. Take into your account the artistic resources of light, when appearing as shade in chiaroscuro, or when existing in the form of colour; think of the quite infinite gradations of expression possible by the fining away of tints, and you see what an instrument is ready for use. You can now express those *nuances* of character, those steps and stages of spiritual process, that waxing and waning, flushing and fading, aspect of development which the Christian impulse has set agoing, and which Christian sympathy and its insinuation of love have made us feel in the history of heart and soul.

These shades, stages, and phases of process in the struggle of the soul, and in the growth of the character, were almost entirely hidden from even the Jewish saint, as well as the modern and manifold variety in the kinds of spiritual excellence.

2. This brings us to another striking feature of painting as compared with the classic art in general and sculpture in particular—its variety, its individuality, its power of expressing particular character, and shades of character. Take any of those cartoons of Raphael; compare it with any group of antique art. What variety of feature, of expression, of attitude, of character, passion, and action. To what does this correspond in Christianity? To the stress and value which that faith lays upon the individual soul and its history. That soul acquired in the Christian creed quite an infinite significance and worth. And the tendency went beyond the individual man, and gave some of this huge importance to individual things. Hence, partly, the great realistic movement in modern art. The slightest objects and phases of Nature were felt to be indispensable parts of a system which was infinite in its range, and of a care which numbered the very hairs of our head. And then along with the delicacies and *nuances* of Art we have, in due time, the microscopic side of science, and its loving interest in the infinitely small as the counterpart of the infinitely great. Now this accession of interest in the steps of natural process, the multiplicity of natural objects, the shades of human development, the

variety of human character, all the poetic, pathetic, tragic ebb and flow of human existence and experience were made representable by the new powers of light, shade, and colour. Again the mighty names of Raphael and Rembrandt come to mind. Nature, as it were, was reflected, not as still, but as instinct with emotion and life. Reality became mobile as even metaphysic has become vitalist. This applies to both external nature and human nature. We saw in dealing with Greek art that it had not the power of expression, in the rich, interesting, and modern sense of the word. The faces of the statues were representations, not of a particular character, or situation, or emotion, but of a type, a type of ideal beauty. They were 'icily regular, splendidly null.' They avoided the disturbance of particular emotion or even action. They were (like the reposeful gods, or the poseful youths) calm, and superior to the warmest sympathies of life. That self-poised, *nil admirari*, poised-beside-their-nectar ideal was the culmination of Greek art. It was the calm of abstraction, and therefore of unreality, which easily becomes affectation. It was only, on the other hand, when Christian art abandoned that ideal, when she turned from the vapid repose of traditional types, when, led by Giotto, that Rembrandt of an earlier age, she took to a loving realism in human life and Bible story, and began to infuse the vraisemblance of human emotion and situation into subject, face, and figure —it was then that she started on her great career to reach her height of power. And we see the best fruit of this tendency in the art of portraiture, a department of painting in which, as in landscape, we are at this day little, if any, behind the greatest masters of the past. And the cause of our success there no doubt lies in the extraordinary and sympathetic interest we take to-day in man as man, in individual persons. The ignoble side of this tendency is to be found in the personalities of a certain journalism, the cheap gossip of the society papers, and the triviality of interest and intelligence which has lost for Art, as for Religion, so much public respect and influence.

A whole lecture might be given to the great and saving influence of Biblical realism in Art, especially in the cases I have named—those of Giotto and Rembrandt. We have seen how Art gained as the grandiose stories of martyrs and saints were replaced by the realistic episodes of Scripture, as it became a people's book; how a pagan naturalism became a Christian realism as egoist passion was replaced by pity and love. Life was not only felt, but felt more preciously and kindly, as the light of the Kingdom of God replaced the glamour of the Church. The light that fell on life became more than the mere lambency of spirituality playing on matter; it became the light of a piercing and positive redemption, a definite faith at close quarters with the reality of human life, in its pathos, tragedy, and sin, personal need met by personal salvation through a personal Redeemer in His personal crisis of the Cross. God's loving heart felt its way to human hearts. Personality came to close quarters with personality. The soul did not need to dress in Sunday attire to appear before God, as in the Mass, nor be introduced to Him by a priestly official. The real and present God came and blessed real daily life with a love and grace in which there was no difference between bond or free, male or female, foul or fair, lovely or coarse. The new sun shone upon the evil and the good, the beautiful and the plain. And, as has been said, Rembrandt's feeling in this kind went as deep as the Gothic spires pierced high. As a son of the world who had tasted all its passion to the deep, he found the Passion of Christ to be the core of all religious life and expression.

This power of sympathetic particularisation, so inherent in painting, so possible to it with its flexible media of colour and shade, appears in respect of external nature in the art of landscape. When a flat surface was substituted for the massive projection of sculpture, it became clear that the chief figure could not be made to fill the whole of the canvas and monopolise the whole field of vision. A large area was left which had to be filled up; and man had to be presented, not stark and sole, but as he is set in a world of context which the modern mind found vaster and vaster. That in itself was an invitation to throw in a variety of detail, to add surroundings to the central figure, to place it in a harmonious setting, and yet preserve the effect of unity throughout the whole. As soon as this was proposed, the whole field of art was enlarged. The human figure was not now of sole importance. Indeed, a morbid asceticism came in here, to add its evil influence to other and better forces tending in the same direction. The nude figure became a horror, and the spectacle of it a suggestion of the devil. It was then either swathed in bandages, as in some of the Byzantine types, or clothed in drapery, upon which a great deal of detail was lavished, while much grace was infused into the lines of its folds. Then the background, which at first was gilt, was filled in with rude landscape, first of a crude symbolical sort out of all perspective, and only gradually becoming more natural, and more in the key of the central figures. Gradually the curtain, so to speak, became the picture, the background was pushed forward, the human figures and incidents were submerged, the scenery became the spectacle, and landscape art took the noble place which it has had for the last two centuries. It is notable that it was chiefly developed in the German, Dutch, and English schools, in the Teutonic race, with its freedom and fidelity, its faculty for spiritual truth and realistic detail, its ponderous but precious painstaking in an ample air, and its sense of God in the nooks and folds of common life. Landscape art is the most modern department of that genius in Art, and in a special way it is the product of the Christian Revelation.

I use the word revelation with some emphasis here. There are the two modes of conceiving the relation of God and Nature. One sees all Nature running up into God. It generalises and makes abstractions. That is philosophy, the classic way of regarding the relation. It rises and leaves detail and expression behind. In the process of abstraction it strips away detail as cumbersome, and it deals with types and ideas. Such is the quality of Greek art. It is abstract. It is apotheosis. The other mode of viewing the relation sees, not all Nature running up into God, but God running down into all Nature. That is to particularise, to give divine value to individuals, without isolating them, to approach, place, and prize details, to love them in themselves because charged with divinity and knit in the whole. That is the way of Religion rather than of Philosophy, the way of Revelation; and it is the quality of Christian art. It is incarnation. It has given rise to landscape, with its vast variety and its inspiration of unity.

3. This brings me to the next feature which links painting with the Christian spirit—the feature of sacrifice and its consequent life and unity. I have spoken of the vast variety introduced into Art by its new power of expressing fine phases of soul or sense. I have linked that with the penetrating spirit of Christianity, its interest in 'these little ones,' the value it lays on the individual, and the fine sympathy with which it enters into the ebb and flow of the heart's tides. But how is it that this huge increase of variety does not end in a vaguer chaos. Multiply objects and interests merely, and you do more than increase confusion. With the new freedom there must enter a new law, or an old law in an application so vast as to

be virtually new. There must enter the law of subordination, sacrifice, perspective, to quell atomic self-assertion. The new multiplicity of artistic subjects can remain artistic only by each serving all the rest, and subsisting in that bond of sacrifice and service which holds outward nature together. As Christianity gave infinite expansion to the doctrine of the Cross, the principle of sacrifice, so that same principle came to be the condition of the best and choicest developments of Christian art. Take one of Turner's great landscapes. What do you find there? The most absolute and exact accuracy of detail in the representation of each object? No. If we look close we see the small human figures, for instance, in the landscape to be mere dabs of colour with no effort at exactness of form. How is this tolerable? Why did Ruskin not send the artist promptly and angrily back to a drawing master? Because that sacrifice of formal exactitude is demanded by the position the figure holds in the whole scene. Greatness involves self-erasure. It quells sharp obtrusion. The figures, in the presence of the vast unity of the landscape, in the presence, too, of the emotion with which the landscape has been charged by the painter's soul—in such a presence the figures must limit and sacrifice their self-assertion. They must not here stand out in the isolation of their particular being. They must subside, melt, and flow into the great outward unity in which they are held. And, indeed, such is the effect in actual vision. When you look at a wide landscape, you can take it in as a scene only on condition that the various objects part with their sharpness of definition, and pass with a fine roughness into the general effect. And therefore it is possible for painting, at the very moment when it is exhibiting the still life of outward nature, to convey also that constant yet invisible flux of change which science tells us is for ever going on in the world. The repose of Nature has to modern eyes for its condition an infinite mobility and energy (not without its moral aspect), which is deeper than mere action, and which the pagan never contemplated in his calmness and grace. There is a life, a unity, and a universality, therefore, about painting and its compositions resting upon this law of sacrifice, and possible only by its means. It is not only, nor chiefly, in great altar-pieces of the Crucifixion that Art bears witness to the power of the Cross, just as it is not in the heroic moments and scenes of our own life that for the most part we have to show forth the Lord's death. I would observe, in passing, that the seamy side of this tendency is the submersion of the soul in the cosmos, and that reign of monism which is in such paradoxical conjunction to-day with the worship of the superman.

The same thing which I have shown in landscape might also be shown in the fondness of painting for groups and compositions, as opposed to the solitary figures which are the *métier* of sculpture and the condition of its calm. The great ancient sculptors do not delight in groups with a multitude of figures in an organic unity. The Laocoön is here quite different from the processional crowd on the Elgin Marbles; and it came as sculpture was ready to pass away. The one unity they knew was the unity of the citizen individual; the unity of spiritual brotherhood they had not yet reached. And so they had not the power of spreading one great emotion in an artistic way through a variety of persons in one work of art. If we compare the cartoons of Raphael with the nearest approach to them in sculpture—the Elgin bas-reliefs (which are half pictures) from the friezes of the Parthenon—we may see the difference between an artistic group as painting could realise it and the mere concourse of splendid figures and vivid action which was all that sculpture could reach. Modern sculpture, from the early Italians downward, has done more in this new direction; but that is simply because modern sculpture has felt those picturesque influences which belong to the Christian time, and has abandoned much of the purely statuesque quality which makes ancient sculpture supreme in its limited kind.

4. In this connection there has been noted another feature of the painting as distinct from the statue, which shows how much more dependent the former is on the sympathy which binds individuals into unity. The picture must be looked at from a single point of view to get its full effect, whereas you must go all round the statue; at least the statue is much more independent of any particular attitude on your part towards it. It stands

out as a self-assertive thing by itself. It is indifferent about you. The picture, on the contrary, makes an appeal to you, calls you into its confidence, says to you, ' If you would judge me right, stand here, view me thus. If you are wrong, I shall be wrong. If you are right, I shall be right.' The picture is painted with a view to the spectator. There is a rapport. The spectator is always, as it were, by the artist's side and in his thought. The statue, on the contrary, is more independent of him. It is more self-sufficient, more stoical— in a word, Greek. So that in the picture the central effect is not only in sympathy and harmony with its surroundings, but it also draws into its field the spectator, makes him, as it were, part of the whole unity, and gives him the distinction of being included like itself in the artistic world.

And there is still another aspect in which the picture makes appeal to the spectator as the statue does not. It works by means of illusion. That is, it produces its effect by a spiritual, a psychological, process, a kind of faith which bears down and silences the contradiction of sense. Thus I have already said that the picture differs from the statue in being on the flat. But its effect depends on the success with which we are made to believe that it is otherwise, that it is no flat surface, but a field of distance and density. The statue really stands out; the picture only seems to. Our senses tell us that it is merely a flat surface we are looking at; but our whole enjoyment of the art depends on our giving the lie to sense, even to common-sense, and living in the momentary faith that the lines are really vistas, the angles really corners, and the curves really spherical. It is within our own spirit that the truth after all lies. The sensuous reality is quite different, and quite tame, and powerless. And this corresponds, not only with a Kantian creed, but with the inwardness and spirituality of Christianity—which teaches us that the outward and sensuous is but a reflection of spiritual reality, not reality itself, which is in the soul.

Once more, we are brought by painting into a rapport with the soul and genius of the painter, to which we are not invited by the sculptor's works. We get more of the artist. The peculiar genius of Turner shines through those landscapes of his much more than the specific quality of Phidias through his statues. Here painting approaches music and poetry, which aim at placing us, with as little of the intervening and obscuring medium as possible, in complete sympathy with what the artist feels and sees.

5. Finally, we have in the depth and warmth contained in colour a fit vehicle of the intensity and passion of love in Christianity—love holiest and most human too. We have entered, if not a brighter, at any rate a richer and more wondrous, world than the Greeks knew. We might think that with their limpid and sunny climate, their varied landscape, and their quick natural soul, the Greeks should have been masters of colour, and their literature at least full of the sense of its

varied depths. But it is not so. I have already reminded you that no words give more trouble to the student of Homer than the adjectives for colour. The same term seems to be applied to objects the most diverse in hue, and it appears often impossible to settle a definite sense which it shall always and clearly bear. Gladstone once printed a paper maintaining that, in Homer's time at least, the sense of colour had not developed, and he supported his position with all his great Homeric learning. It seems a strange thing, but something like it appears to be true. Whether the Greeks of Homer's time saw colour or not, as a people they were comparatively careless about it. It was not the hue of coloured objects which attracted them, but their brightness. 'They did not care for colour for its own sake.' It was a sense of light rather than of colour that they had. 'They looked through the hue to its cause.' Where we see a glow they saw rather the gleam. Ruskin connects this colour-blindness with the shadow of Fate which hung over Greek life, which is the background of their sad tragedies, and is associated with the absence of any faith in Immortality. It may be so. It shows how sight itself suffers for want of faith and love, how essential the vision of the inward eye and the life of the inward heart are to the full vision even of the outward world.

In the mediæval heyday of faith in love it was otherwise. The earth bloomed forth in copious variety and new depths of hue; and no pigment was too brilliant, too hopeful, too cheerful for the utterance of the age's spiritual outlook. The old symbolic rose—an emblem among the Jews also, who seem, like all Orientals, to have been quicker to see colour than the Greeks—was revived with a new glow in its petals, and a new suggestion in its abysmal flame. It became for Dante the emblem of all the wealth of eternity. The most powerful of colours became the most frequent in art; and the excessive, and to us often distasteful, way in which the blood of Christ appears in old paintings is not due simply to crudeness of taste, but, in part at least, to the action of taste, to the power of deep and significant colour which it lent to the symbolism of Art. This hue—always appropriated to the expression of love—became deeper and deeper in its Christian use. The warmth, the passion, the ecstasy of complete devotion found a reflection in this massive colour; and on the rose's wealth of cumulative and concentric glory—fold on fold retiring richly, reluctantly, and with reverent obeisance from a central source—mediæval thought gazed and pored till it found there an image of the host of heaven and assembly of the redeemed, washed with blood, and crowded round the altar-throne, whereon was the semblance of a lamb as it had been slain. So also the depth of blue was seized to express the simplicity, serenity, and truthfulness of a soul so pious, true, and sweet as the Virgin was held to have been.

Orthodox Protestantism has not been artistic in the direction of painting. It has had, through

Calvin, the French and Greek tendency to intellect and the Greek insensibility to the warm and coloured side of life, as well as the civic and social instinct of Greece. Through Calvin it followed the modern scientific tendency to construe the world rather than represent it; while through Luther and Teutonism it had a bias to the homely, and a grasp, often gross, of the obtrusive realisms of life, as well as a prior bias to music, where Protestantism has been inward and spiritual with the best. But still more, it has had to contend for the primacy of the ethical in life and salvation. It has been too engrossed with the moral conflict of life, with sin, and the escape from it by inward victory, to have its interest free to devote to the lines of beauty and the glow of colour. It has often been charged to Protestantism that when it parted from Catholicism, it lost the power of intense devotion and refined absorption in its worship. It lost in faith the spirit of love. Its prayer was poor, its ceremonial bald, its fabrics meagre, and its thought cold. There is some truth in the charge. It has become too individual and self-absorbed, perhaps. The saving of the single soul has been more to it at times than the redemption of the Church and the world. It has unduly depreciated works—and works of art among the rest—in order to enhance the value of a faith which too often fell a victim to the intellectualism it inherited from mediæval Catholicism. That may perhaps be true, but if it is, the worth of knowing it is this—that we may revise our idea of faith, and cherish a nobler hope,

PAINTING

and look forward to a time when the outward and the inward, having each in isolation grown larger, shall again unite:

> When world and soul, according well,
> Shall make one music as before,
> But vaster.[1]

Protestant ethic and Catholic comprehensiveness may be fused into some union nobler than as yet has been, in the course of dealing with the social crisis of the future. For the finest art has in the past been compatible with the worst social conditions and the most grievous oppression of the poor. Of all Europe the land of Art has been the cruel land. And it is such social conditions that at last have brought Art low. But with the social problem solved, and the Church united in the doing of it, piety may regain its old power to exult and rejoice rather than wrestle and wander and weep, and be able to speak forth in shapes and hues a life as deep, rich, varied, and prolific as in a time gone by.

[1] In Memorium, prologue (altered).

VI

CHRISTIANITY AND PAINTING—II

The History

THE progress of Art on the whole has been, not in the nature of abstraction, or speculation, but in the nature of revelation. It has not risen from earth to heaven. It has come down with its light from heaven to earth. Early painting was distinctively religious; the last is distinctively natural. So far as the history of the art goes, it began in faith, it ends in glorified sight. It rose in the saved soul, it ends in transfigured sense (if I may use that expression with no gross implication, but in a philosophical way). The light which issued from the soul now shines on the world at large, and men see its glory but forget its source. The beam from heaven which first lighted the soul is now lighting the world, till the seeing soul forgets itself and its own destiny, entranced for the time by the manifold splendours of the revelation that is without. The glow has slowly broadened down through centuries. Where they used to paint the beauty of holiness, they now paint the holiness of beauty. Painting began with the soul as the realm of God; it ends with the universe as the realm of power and law, beauty and order. It began by seeing God in the face of man; it ends, so far, by seeing Him in the face of Nature. Art, cradled and reared in Religion, has in these latter days been taken in hand by science. The Royal Society is next door to the Academy, and under the same roof—which is an allegory. I am not complaining. I am only stating what seems the case in regard to the historical development of Art. And I am not saying that Art is irreligious because it has ceased to be distinctively Christian, any more than is the case with thought. For one may cease to call himself a Christian, and yet remain a very religious man. The very naturalism and realism of recent art is, through the action of religion, a whole world different from the naturalism of classic Greece. There is that in Turner's ' Vale of Tempe ' which no ancient Greek saw; the classic subjects of Titian or Raphael are much more than classic in their treatment, spirit, and effect; and Swinburne's classicism is more romantic than classic. Art certainly did not cease to be religious when it ceased to be ecclesiastical. It did not cease to be in the large sense Christian, except when it became degraded as Art, and had little else to show than sensuous fulness or soulless inhumanity. Perhaps the best thing to say is that at present the truly spiritual is in abeyance, as for a thousand years and more the truly natural was in abeyance, till the great mediæval masters arose. Man goes on two feet, and to move forward one must always in turn be behind. At present the right foot is to the rear.

The art of painting in Christian times may be divided into three great periods corresponding to the three great peoples who contributed to form the modern world. Leaving the Semitic family out of account, as not of originative power in this region, we have the three great elements blended in Christianity as we have it to-day, the Greek, the Roman, and the Teutonic. The special contribution of each of these races may be regarded as an independent factor, apart from the spiritual inspiration which Christianity offered them as a centre and stimulus. The infusion of the Teutonic (and I may add the Keltic) element into the Roman empire in the Dark Ages is to be reckoned as a concomitant cause, along with the Christianity which appropriated that element, of the great outburst of fresh life and activity which slowly issued in the Middle Ages, and gave the arts their birth. To this I shall return. I go on to say that the three periods, in correspondence with the three factors named, are the Greek, the Roman, and the Teutonic periods.

So we have:
    I. Byzantine Art.
    II. Italian art.
    III. Flemish, German, and English art.

I. *Byzantine Art.*

The origins of painting in the Christian era were religious. It cannot, indeed, be said that the art sprang from the religion in the same direct way as sculpture flowed from the Greek religion. I have

CHRISTIANITY AND PAINTING

already often enough alluded to Christianity's independence of Art; and I have distinguished it in that respect from the Greek creed, which could not but run into art and culminate there. The great development of Christian art took place only after the infusion of the Teutonic and Keltic races into Christian society, while no such foreign influence intervened to produce sculpture out of Greek paganism. Nevertheless it was Christianity, acting first on the classic peoples, and then on the Transalpine races, which gave the occasion and the inspiration, if not the precise form, for the painting of Christian Europe. The sacred figures and scenes which offered the first invitation and the first subjects to this art gathered round the figure of the Incarnate God in Jesus Christ. Painting sprang from the desire to give form to the object of the supreme passion—which was not the man Jesus so much as the God who, by Incarnation as a Man, had made humanity immortal. Besides its new ideas, Christianity gave rise to two new worships—Christ and Mary—to say nothing of the adoration of saints and angels; and this had a powerful effect on Art. So that we might almost say that but for the belief in the Incarnation, and the subtle action of its principle, the art of painting at least would never have come to more than it achieved in classic times. The Greeks and Romans cultivated it with no small success, but the moral and social corruption of paganism had already told on the excellence of their painting when Christianity began to grow; and we can still see both features on Pompeian walls. The Christians of the Apostolic age had no connection with art so far as we know. How should they, with the crack of doom, the winding up of all things, the burning and purifying of all earth's products momentarily at hand? But soon, as the Lord's coming (in the sense they expected) was delayed, their thoughts began to widen, and their sympathies with the world they had left to grow again. The Catacombs give us valuable evidence that the charm of classic art was not wholly ignored by the blithe faith of those subterranean saints who sang in the dark. Recent researches have brought to light, not only rude symbols like the ship, the fish, the crown, the palm, the lamb, the peacock, and the door, but representations of Old Testament scenes symbolical of Christian truths and doctrines, *e.g.* Noah in the Ark, the sacrifice of Isaac, the sin of our first parents, Moses striking the rock, and so on. These reverent believers avoided, though not entirely, the direct representations of scenes in Christ's life. They set Him forth in one or other sort of symbol. Many of the figures in the Old Testament scenes are both drawn and painted with a grace, vigour, and classic beauty which, Kugler says, approach very near to the wall paintings of the best period of the Roman Empire. But in one part they offer a strong contrast to those mural paintings, as we see when we compare this subterranean Christianity with the subterranean paganism of Pompeii. Of course there is nothing wanton or unchaste; but also there is no gloom or despair.

CHRISTIANITY AND PAINTING

The angel of death is not a sad genius with torch reversed; and the figures are modestly and gracefully draped from neck to heel. There is no effort at verisimilitude in these pictures in the Catacombs. The dresses are not Jewish, but Roman; and many of the smaller symbols are classical, with a Christian meaning infused. Where the figure of Christ is introduced, there is no effort at portraiture. He is youthful, fresh, and joyous—an ideal image of the everlasting youth of the faith. He is the projection, the genius, of the religion, rather than its founder and historic head. In this art we are little beyond the symbolic stage. The object was merely to suggest, to strike the charged rock of the believer's heart, as it were, which poured forth love and faith at a touch. But when Christianity emerged from the Catacombs, efforts at portraiture began to abound. It is then that we find what profess to be likenesses of sacred personages, especially of Christ Himself. The Church believed Luke to have been a painter, and Nicodemus a sculptor; and they further deemed themselves to possess authentic works from their hands. They treasured also pictures said not to have been made with hands, but descended from heaven; and amongst other relics was the famous representation of the face of Christ left on the handkerchief of St. Veronica. These paintings gave the type of feature which all art down to Raphael, more or less, observed, especially in depicting the Saviour. The special type assigned to Him is thought by many to be of Gnostic origin.

K

Gradually, however, the blithe and cheerful aspects of the faith fell into the background, and the solemnity and earnestness which it drew from contact and battle with the world took their place in Art. The 'splendour in the grass and the glory in the flower' passed into a more stern and, in a sense, more exalted and grave tone of mind. The Church had mixed with the affairs of the world, and, in the compromises and adjustments of policy, had lost much of the tender grace, sweet simplicity, and ingenuous veracity of its first years. The result appears in art. The grace and beauty, borrowed from the antique and inspired with a new freshness, is lost. A sense of awe and distance thrusts itself into the relation between Christ and man, and it submerges the intimacies of a simpler reverence. The sense of Christ's divine nature grows. The deep feeling which kept the Christians of the Catacombs from representing the Passion, or even the Cross, of Christ on their walls gives way to a deeper sense of His work and place, and crosses and figures of the dying Saviour begin to appear. At first He is alive and erect on the Cross as if to indicate that He could not die. Step by step the horror deepens. Death and its agonies are spread over the figure, the realism taking sometimes a very naïve form. For instance, the blood, pouring from the wound in the side on the spectators' heads, indicates the direct efficacy of the atonement. The old gentleness and sweetness has vanished from the face. All that is triumphantly divine ceases to be felt, and only a human woe

CHRISTIANITY AND PAINTING

remains. Materiality and severity assume the upper hand; and from the gross agonies of the crucified body, art passes to represent Christ, in the hour of exultation and nemesis, as an awful judge, restrained from severe punishment only by the intercession of the Virgin. These steps, which were quite gradual and covered centuries, were realised chiefly in the Eastern Church. And the most potent influence in the way of mischief was the blighting predominance of the priestly caste. I have already pointed out how things divine and living became dogmatised and petrified in that Church, and how development was checked, and corrupted into outbreaks of violence, arresting a culture which was really there, and alternating with years of sloth and spiritual death. The eyes of Art, too, became glazed. They no longer had the quickness of life, or saw the grace of natural ways. We found already that the Greek tendency in Art was towards types of beauty rather than individuals. And so the Greek end of the Church, as the religious life sank away under priestly and imperial rule, became typical in its art. The old type of face, the old type of attitude, situation, and symbol, became fixed and conventional, like the old type of doctrine; or, if it changed, changed only for the worse to express the ideas of monkery, asceticism, and physical torture. Saints in pictures became more and more like mummies. Any resemblance to Nature became increasingly a sin. The figures were more like rude carvings than paintings—lank, stiff, and stark. There was no melting, no chiaroscuro, no perspective. Mosaic, with its broad and symbolistic effects, and manuscript illumination, with its barbaric wealth of colour and poor resources of expression, were almost the only forms in which Art existed. Art became artifice, soul vanished under the pressure of a timid tyranny; and over the whole field was spread distortion, vapidity, and the ghastliness of mental death. It was not only a mere symbolism, it was a dead symbolism, a dried flower, which only witnessed to a life and freshness once there, but long gone. Such was Byzantine painting as it stands on the walls of basilicas and the margins of manuscripts up till the eleventh century. It ought, however, in fairness to be said, that occasionally there is a suggestion of solemnity and depth in the figure, though little of beauty and love.

II. *Italian Art*

The art of the West during this time was but little better. It was less ghastly, but more gross and barbaric in its effects. It witnessed less to spiritual death than to an undeveloped and unchastened rudeness of natural life. It was the twilight of Art both in East and West; but in the East it was the evening twilight, in the West it was the morning. There was promise with the West. The type was less oppressive. There were indications of some individuality and vigour, and a lingering sense of spiritual victory kept within some bounds the tendency to dwell on physical agony and material realism. The crucifixions of

CHRISTIANITY AND PAINTING

this date show the difference between East and West. 'The Eastern Church, with its fondness for bodily anguish, represented the figure on the Cross with all the weight of the body hanging down, swollen waist, the relaxed knees bent to the left, the head drooping, and the face marked with all the torment of a cruel death. The Western Church, on the other hand, had far fewer representations of the scene at all, but when it was presented the figure was upright, and the whole aspect of it was invested rather with the expression of spiritual victory than of physical agony.' It is to the spread of Byzantine influences over the West when the Greek Empire broke up that we must ascribe much of the artistic horror which we find in the West.

In the Dark Ages, the art of the East was in death, that of the West was but in germ. But in the darkness of that time there was growing a power which, quickened by the spirit of Christianity, was to step forth and give to Art such a fulness of free and beauteous life as she never had enjoyed before. I dealt in the last lecture with its Christian principle. I deal now with the historic occasion and ethnical base which gave that spirit outward shape. The two great Transalpine nationalities, the Keltic and Teutonic, had already poured their fresh vigour into Rome; and now came the time when their spiritual contribution was to emerge, take power, and reign. It is not possible, to me at least, to trace in historic sequence the threads of this new influence amid classic feeling and thought. It must be enough to recognise that it was there, and to give it the honour that is its due. What is the grand feature whose development means the progress of Christian painting from the tenth or eleventh century to Raphael? It is the feature of individualisation, of characterisation. It is, like the recent life-of-Jesus movement, the rejection of typical faces and conventional situations, and the substitution of real human faces and emotions, and of probable attitudes and relations. The history of Christian painting is the history of a progressive Incarnation, the divine spirit of faith and love passing, with increasing force, truth, and beauty, into the inner conditions of our human soul and life. It is the history of a reconciliation growingly real and intimate between God and man, the divine nature and the human. It is the elaboration in time's detail of a unity established eternally, and once for all effected for history in Christ. The feature of individualisation, veracity, attention to individual character and situation, that is the prime and growing feature of the great Italian art up to Raphael. But now what is the conspicuous feature of the Teutonic nationalities, the feature which they express alike in their primitive political constitution, and in their great contribution to the world's religion—in their free citizenship on the one hand and in their Protestantism on the other? Is it not this very feature of personality—the individual as faithful and free, unbound at last by anything lower than truth and conscience?

CHRISTIANITY AND PAINTING

This feature of the Teutonic peoples allied itself with the Roman sense of political order, and both received a new consecration and impulse from Christianity; and we see the artistic side of the union in the realistic development of Italian or religious Art, in the great international society of a Church, with all its ideal charm; but for the invasion of the Teuton Italy would not have had an art, any more than England would have been free.

But there is another side to the Teutonic character. It combines with its realism an exalted and often mystic idealism. You see it in its Teutonic home in that school of mystics who, headed by Tauler and Eckhart, preceded the Reformation. This is an element which found a kindred soil in certain forms of classic thought. It allied itself easily with the tendencies that made Plato and his later Christian disciples; it finds an echo at least in the Fourth Gospel; and it founded the schools of Alexandria. As classic idealism united with Christianity to form the thought of the Eastern Church, and much of the theology also of the West, so Teutonic idealism, adding its new religious vigour to both these, found artistic expression in that sublime and mystic quality which pervades and distinguishes Italian art. The classical element must, however, have gone for much in this conjunction. For we find in purely Teutonic art the realism getting the upper hand, and the idealism often quite lost.

But besides its truthful reality, exalted and controlled by a spiritual ideal, Italian art had another supreme quality—that of extreme grace, elegance, and beauty of form. Now, apart from the grace and beauty of holiness which form its spiritual and Christian content, where did this feature come from ? From two sources, one of which seems certain, the other probable. First, and certainly, from the influence of the classic sense of beauty, grace, and formal perfection. Secondly, and possibly, from the influence of the Keltic or Gallic faculty for charm, elegance, and all that is suggested, especially in colour, by the word magic, the influence which contributed so much to Gothic architecture, with its origins in Northern France. This magical element of essential beauty in colour, uniting with the element of grace or formal beauty in drawing, the Keltic uniting with the purely classic, may account historically for the third great feature of Italian art, its grace, its spell, its melody, its pure beauty. But here again much depends, so far as the Keltic element is concerned, on the admixture with the other influences. For the Keltic race, with all its sense of colour and magic, has not produced a pictorial art of its own.

It is in Raphael (say 1500 A.D.) that all these features meet and mingle for the perfection of great Christian art. It boots nothing to enter into his genealogy, and seek to trace in his extraction the qualities I have named. He was the product rather of a great social era than of a particular family line, and the influences which made him were seething in the social milieu of centuries before him. He absorbed and kindly mixed the elements

CHRISTIANITY AND PAINTING

of a richly laden world. He was in the line of a vast artistic movement which began centuries before he was born.

At the beginning of the Middle Ages there was one great historical idea which had much to do with the origin of high Christian art. It was the dream of the Kingdom of God—the Holy Roman Empire—as entertained by the great Gregory, and fostered by many a like spirit in his wake. This empire was to reflect in the government of the earth the rule of God over the world. There was to be but one power—God, Christ; and the Pope was to be His vicar. The spirit of God and the ethic of the faith was to fill and mould every department of human action, no less than every region of human abode. It was the plain duty, therefore, of the vicegerent of God in this great comprehensive Church to take no mean account of the artistic side of human energy. To this end he must first bind under a spiritual authority and a strong order the whole of shattered Europe, and so make that quietness and confidence which is the strength of Art. Such pacification was in fact secured; and a portion of the newly awakened energy of the human spirit was accordingly turned into the channel of Art. Religion would occupy this land also, and use its victories for the decoration of her triumph. And Art, thus raised and encouraged, was allowed a freedom which thought longed for in vain. The same danger to the faith was not dreaded from the artists as from the thinkers (though the artists, as thinkers, had much to do with the catastrophe which came). It was not in the shape of Art, but in that of philosophy and its dialectic, that the new freedom was expected to break with the Church. Art, therefore, had a scope and an encouragement, both from the rulers and the ruled, which had much to do with its rapid and brilliant success. There was no Academy, and no professional guild. The artists were an independent clergy, who were in the closest and most vital contact with the people among whom they lived; the more especially as the time had not yet come when people of culture were widely at variance with the popular creed. A common religious faith, by many of the greatest artists truly and ardently held and lived, spread coherence and sympathy through the great social organism, to a degree which made a free and lofty art both possible and powerful. To the unity of the Church corresponded the internationality in the style of Art. The great difference from modern art is that the mediæval had a *Weltanschauung*. It inhabited a unitary world of thought resting on a dogma, while the modern world, repudiating dogma, loses also in that surrender such a command of life and the world as goes with great art, and places it level with science or faith. The mediæval art had the note of authority, which, in some shape or other, is inseparable from spiritual (or any) greatness. This dream of the Kingdom of God, so noble, yet so impracticable, so pure and high in purpose, and yet so mixed and tainted in effect, though it did not issue in a lasting empire of Europe, yet did spread

CHRISTIANITY AND PAINTING 143

through Europe a vast if vague sense of corporate unity, which all subsequent efforts at a European concert have failed to reproduce. And it put a religious seal upon energies that needed some such high sanction to help and guide them from confusion to light. It was the early years of European manhood, and a tutor and governor was not to be dispensed with yet.

The first beginnings of the new reality and life in Art, under the shadowing wing of Rome, were made from Florence; and the first conspicuous name is that of Cimabue (1240-1302). His greatest work—a Madonna—is still to be seen; and having seen it we can guess at the wretched poverty of preceding art as we read of the popular enthusiasm with which this picture, so primitive to us, was greeted, when carried in festive procession from the painter's study to the church where it was to hang. The traveller in the desert will spring with a cry to a very tiny bush of green; and the Borgo Allegri, as the quarter ever since has been named, records the excitement of a people famished for one touch of Nature and athirst for one line of reality in Art. But the great name in early Italian painting is that of Giotto. It was Cimabue's greatest feat when he found Giotto in the field and took him from following the sheep. The older painter's greatest work was the young artist he made. Rude and imperfect as Giotto's works also seem to us to-day, yet there is in them a huge advance both in technique and ideas. Oil painting as yet was not, but, instead of the stiff and dull wax of the Byzantines, Giotto mixed his colours with clear vegetable sap. His drawing became more graceful, especially in the drapery, where the long folds he introduced corresponded to the long perpendicular line of the contemporary Gothic architecture. He introduced new types of face as he strove to infuse into the features what he really saw among men and women around him. He became, in a word, natural; which is to say that he became less ecclesiastical, and more truthful and religious. He was a man of shrewd and independent character, and of true religious feeling, unburdened with an excessive veneration for the priests and clergy among whom he lived. He painted the present, and not the past. And he had great help in this effort from a tendency developing in the then Church to canonise men and women who were almost contemporary. The spiritual world was brought near, and the truly marvellous was felt to lie neither in an accessible past nor in the future of a post-mortem existence. 'The living, the living shall praise Thee, as I do this day.' There was in all this perhaps some loss of the solemnity of an earlier and ruder art, just as a cloistered and fugitive virtue may be more nobly severe than the truer and richer ethic of one who has lived in close fellowship and kind contact with varied life. But far more was gained than lost in fidelity, reality, sympathy, humanity, and grace.

The subjects of art were still entirely religious. It was the incidents of Scripture, especially now of the Gospels, that were thought worthy of

CHRISTIANITY AND PAINTING

enshrinement in Art—these along with personifications of the Christian virtues. But, conformably to the spirit of naturalness and humanity, attention was fixed as it had not been before on the human side of Christ's character, the Nativity, the childhood, the Virgin Mother, and all those links which bind the sacred history with what is tender and homely in the experience of the heart. Nothing could be more sweet and homely then Giotto's frescoes of these events, as at Padua. The death of Christ was set forth rather in its touching and moving than in its sublime and victorious aspect—which was largely a consequence of the enthusiasm lately roused by the work of St. Francis in the human and compassionate side of the Gospel life.

We are here made to feel from another side what I have already spoken of as the humanising and ethicising influence of a realistic literature upon Art. I have suggested the effect of the Bible in breeding the new ethical spirit which really underlay the outbreak of mediæval art. But I have not alluded, as I do now, to the parallel effect of the rise and spread among all classes of the national poetry and literature of the West. This had, perhaps, more effect upon the origins of mediæval (and so of all modern) art than the rediscovery of Greek culture had upon its close at the Renaissance. There was in that popular literature a vigour, a realism, a humanism, a tenderness and a humour which deeply affected the whole culture of the time, and affected it in a way more or less hostile to the ecclesiastical tradition and style. It was lay, lusty, and racy. It had grown up in a stout independence of priest and Church, often indeed in bitter, satirical antagonism to them in the name of human nature with its worth and freedom. It was the counterpart of the work of Robert Burns so near our own time. But yet it had no idea of any breach in principle with the system or unity of the Church. Like Savonarola or Wycliffe, it was reformatory, but not, like Luther, reformational.

With all the excellences I have named, there were still, of course, in this early art many defects. The drawing for a century yet at least is incorrect. Perspective is ill understood. The figures stand on their toes rather than on their feet, and the backgrounds are only symbolical hints. A rock represents a desert, a tree stands for a wood, and a bluish space with impossible fishes means the sea. 'Yet amid all this ignorance, this imperfect execution, this limited range of power,' says Mrs. Jameson, ' how exquisitely beautiful are some of the remains of this early time, affording, in their simple, genuine grace and lofty, earnest, and devout feeling, examples of excellence which our modern painters begin to feel and understand, and which the great Raphael himself did not disdain to study, and even to copy.'

Giotto's great genius is inadequately represented by what we have of his work, and it is realisable only when we attend to what he did for the development of Art in the conditions of his time. He marks the fourteenth century as Cimabue does the

CHRISTIANITY AND PAINTING 147

thirteenth. Passing to the fifteenth, we remember it by two great but very different names, Fra Angelico and Masaccio. The progressive incarnation of the soul in the natural flesh, experiences, and situations of man was still going on. The religious emotion of the painters does not rise so much higher, especially after Angelico, but the power of expression, and of uniting all the artistic excellences, does. The humane is continually coming to the front of the ecclesiastical, while the divine element does not retire. What we find especially is an increased power of rapt religious expression in the face. Such is Angelico's art. And with that goes an increased rounding of the form generally, with a new truth and expression thrown into the whole body. That is Masaccio's. While Raphael himself never exceeded the purity and completeness of ecstatic devotion which the saint painter of the Florentine cloister poured into the faces of his lamely drawn figures. They melt in the glow of the prayer without which the unworldly artist is said never to have begun to paint; and they are transfigured in the light of that pious inspiration which he believed himself in consequence to possess so fully that he would never alter anything he did lest he should be tampering with the Holy Ghost. It is also said of Angelico that he never painted the sorrows of Christ without weeping. Except Giotto, it was Fra Angelico that first revealed to Art the depths and possibilities of the human face; while Masaccio, devoting himself to the study of anatomy, brought out, for the first time in painting, the truth of the body, and developed the power of light and shade in showing forth its round mass. Never in art has there been a deeper expression, though there has been a more perfect one, of the simple *liebesquellendes Auge*, the pure constancy and tenderness of faithful and sublimated love brimming amid sorrow, wreck, and blight. Both Nature and soul, then, in this century received power; and Art, we may say, as it grew in stature, grew in grace, and in favour with God and man.

But the range of Art was expanding. It remained religious, but the scope and empire of the religion was widened. Not saints alone, even those canonised from near the artist's own time, were now represented. A new class came to the front and to freedom about this time—the citizen or burgher class—the man who does not give his whole life and soul to religion, but comes to his religion from time to time out of a life filled with other interests and thoughts, yet is ready to serve the cause of religion with all his energy and resources when the call arrives. The civic life, like the military life, becomes associated in a harmonious way with the life of religion and the Church; and an alliance is struck between piety on the one side, and, on the other, industry, freedom, commerce, peace, patriotism, courage of a stubborn if not brilliant sort, and the well-to-doness of municipal life. Towers, palaces, and ships appear in the backgrounds of paintings; and in the figures that pay their homage to the sanctities

CHRISTIANITY AND PAINTING 149

of faith are to be found portraits of those powerful burghers, merchants, and civil chiefs who had acquired such an influence on the time. The modern economic age of productive industry was dawning, and modern Europe was beginning to strain at the leash of Rome, or at least to chafe at the control of the Roman curia. Religion was escaping from the Church and passing into life; and the expansion finds an expression in the complexion of contemporary art. We may trace, indeed, some relaxation of intense and abstract piety; but the entrance of the secular element, as it was a feature of civilisation, so was a necessary step towards the perfection of Art. For it must press on, not to a purely transcendent goal, like abstract religion, but to a type of faith more concrete with life and to the complete reconciliation in beauty of the soul and the world. Art, if it do look into heaven, must still stand upon earth. Only the two elements must be further blended than this fifteenth century yet feels them to be.

That fusion was the work of the sixteenth century, the century of the five great masters, viz. Michael Angelo, Leonardo da Vinci, Correggio, Titian, and Raphael—to whom ought, perhaps, be added Tintoretto. The whole fruit of this century is gathered up in Raphael; and the qualities which singly, perhaps, were as strong in others, co-exist in him in a fusion and harmony so entire, in such admirable proportion and exquisite balance, that he becomes the apex and epitome both of his age and of his art. Leonardo brought his genius to

L

bear on the expressive resources of the body, and, by the profound labour of a powerful understanding, acquired a mastery of technique, which, being joined with his artistic insight and his religious sense, advanced painting a long stage in its reality, while losing none of its lofty force. Titian and Correggio developed all the resources of rich and deep colour. But Raphael combined all the painter's gifts in a magical charm and inexpressible beauty which go to the very fountains of feeling, and cover with a complete ease and grace those vast depths of power which in an artist like Michael Angelo stand out gigantic, unchastened, and unsubdued. Truly, when we compare these Madonnas, now the inmates of every home, with the Titanic productions of Michael Angelo, we have the triumph of the weak things of the world over the things which are mighty. Art, Nature, Antiquity, and Religion are gathered up in Raphael, and so balanced that no mannerism is associated with his name. ' In him were united the highest sensibility to religious emotion, the most keen and loving regard to Nature in her living colours and shapes, and a like sense for the beauty of antique art. It was the principle of Greek beauty he grasped. He did not imitate its forms, but he poured its spirit into new and living organs, and he raised it to a height before untouched of expression and character.'

From Raphael Italian art sank and decayed. Ruskin says that in his perfection the decay had already set in, and he is the summit which unites

CHRISTIANITY AND PAINTING 151

the upward slope and the downward. Italy had spent its powers. It could henceforth only imitate one or two other masters. The virtue was gone out of it, and with the corruptions in the Church a corruption crept into Art. The moral force of the Church had gone in the direction of Germany, and lived in the Reformation. Art ceased to be ideal. It became purely natural, but without that power of inward realism which can make naturalistic art truthful and strong. It became false and weak. The removal of the Church's centre of gravity to Spain after the Reformation did give a new life to ideal and religious art there, and several Spanish painters of that time take a very high and worthy place. Foremost among them, of course, is Murillo, who may take rank with all but the very greatest Italians. But the future of painting lay henceforth with another school, the product of another race. It passed from being ideal, mystic, and delicate to being intensely realistic and powerful. The succession passed from the South to the North, from the Italian and Spaniard to the Teuton, to the Fleming, the German, and the Englishman.

III. *Teutonic Art*

The feature of this art, as I have said, is its intense realism, its individuality, its free fidelity of representation, with less care for beauty than for truth, in so far as beauty can be subordinate to truth while remaining Art at all. It is not imaginative in the special sense of that word; it is not ideal, it is not ecstatic. It is penetrative rather than lambent imagination. It is actual, veracious, firm on the solid ground of Nature and man as they palpably are. As the depraved tendency of Italian art was to the sentimental and false, so the lower tendency of this is to the gross. It is the constant temptation and besetting sin of the Teutonic stock—this bias to the vulgar, the stupid, the true which is but the outer or lower half of the truth, the obvious, the earthly, the lusty —*und was uns Alle bändigt, das Gemeine.* The religion of this people searches rather than soars, and is strong rather than fine. They pore, they think, they sing, they work, all with vigour and rigour. Their word is '*Thorough.*' They are deeply alive, indeed, to the inward life of the soul; only it tends to worship of a somewhat inarticulate and tongue-tied sort. They do prize a pure and perfect devotion, yet their faith is broad rather than sublime, and it shows itself rather as illuminating the interests and occupations of the world than transfigured on a mountain top above it. The Virgin, who is in Italian art a maiden, and in Spanish art a queen, is in Teutonic art a matron, and even a dame. The Child looks the son of man rather than the Son of God. And their special artistic power is not sublimity of imagination so much as depth and width of sensibility, with a tendency, in the weaker forms, to sentiment of the domestic rather than the dainty sort.

One striking illustration of the difference between the two types of art is to be found in the

CHRISTIANITY AND PAINTING 153

order of natural character which is taken as the base for religious and imaginative representation. The saint must have, under the saintship, a certain natural character, which in Italian art is of one order and in Teutonic is of another. Now we have two great divisions of natural character to go upon. On the one hand, we have the sweet, gentle, noble, dignified, orderly, and obedient character, the product of an old civilisation, the fruit, it may be, of generations of Christian discipline and worship, but made what it is by no conscious effort on the individual's side. It is such a character as we find in many men and countless women in the middle and upper class—with passion well in hand, but affection ready and free, not self-assertive, but yet not insipid or vapid, with a natural affinity for those elements in Christianity which are its inner charm. There is by nature in such people no bias to the mean, the trivial, the coarse. They do not strive or cry. They are ladies and gentlemen whatever class they belong to. They are not the victims of struggle in their path to the good and true. They are reared in a Church which relieves men of such responsibility. The distortions of passion do not mar their repose and balance of heart and soul. For the graces and beauties of Christianity, as I say, they have a natural affinity, and they pass into the heaven of devotion without a fierce wrestle to escape from their heaven on earth. They move in a world of the refined and the urbane, which descends in its imitations to religious dandyism and æsthetic pose. Such are the natural types on which the Italian painters rear their saints and Virgins. There is a fine harmony between Nature and grace, between the human and the divine. The body, the soul, and the spirit harmoniously blend, and therefore we have in Italian art something like the Greek perfection. We have pain, sorrow, perhaps even repentance, but it is all of a tempered, mellowed, and subdued sort. It is not stormy, fitful, wrapt in the blackness of despair, or torn with the agony of remorse.

But the national type which the Teutonic artist found readiest to his hand was very different. He lived amid a bitter and stern nation, where civilisation came far later than on the Mediterranean shores, where there had never been either a pagan culture or such a Christianity as the Antonine Age; where individuality was strong, obstinate, passionate; where a rough climate bred a wild and masterful character, only by huge effort to be subdued to the gentler way. The order of natural character which the Teutonic artist had for a base was of that sort. It tended to the harsh, the stiff, the gross, and coarsely sinful. Resignation was often possible only after violent struggles, and the powerful will, thwarted in great things, spends itself on little things and becomes trivial, mean, and suspicious. The very piety is apt to be rude and gnarled in these powerful doers. And even when some degree of peace and grace has been reached, the storm of previous passions or generations has left its trace. There are scars of battle which disfigure the features. The wounds received in the rebellion against God, or in the conflict with a rude and almost indomitable self, are not always quite closed or healed. They are often a plague to the creed they profess: narrow, bitter, and intolerant towards others, because they have been the same towards themselves, because the grace of God is a too foreign element still in their souls, and the assimilation will take some generations yet to complete. The reconciliation with God is only partially effected, and the rude soul is still labouring to be reconciled with itself. Such was the natural base which the Teutonic artists had to go upon, and you can see that they were hampered at the outset. Out of their stiff-necked and rebellious generation they could not hope to rear such products of artistic perfection as the Italian masters drew from an old classic culture and a long Christian discipline. They could not set forth such freedom of aspiration, such ease of spiritual movement under the influence of divine grace grown second nature, such a soul's firmament of purity, unbroken, like an Italian sky, by clouds of harsh or sinful memory, and untainted by the smoke of torment from fiery passion or engulfed despair.

Of course I do not dream that all the Teutonic pictures of holy men and women are ungainly and rude. I have been pressing the contrast between two types, and describing the tendencies of each rather than the features. And there are artists of the North little inferior in power and grace to those of the South. The whole development of landscape art, culminating in Turner, is of northern growth, springing in great part from Teutonic individualism and *Gemüthlichkeit*. Of that I spoke in my last lecture. And the painting of domestic or familiar incident, what is called *genre* painting, with its power of humour, tenderness, and fresh naturalness, that, too, is of the North. There is no humour in the great artists I have mostly named. Humour is possible only to minds of a strongly realistic cast, not possible, therefore, to the almost haughty idealism of Italian art, nor to the sentimentalism which is idealism run to seed.

The first Teutonic paintings are the work of the two brothers Van Eyck, who lived in the Netherlands in the first half of the fifteenth century. There are two remarkable facts in connection with them. The first is that the elder, Hubert, was the first to discover, or at any rate to utilise in any fertile way, oil as a vehicle for colour; and he may be called the father of oil-painting. The second is that their art is a sort of special creation, not developing from any ascending series, but 'springing up full statured in an hour.' They are masters unequalled by any of their school in accuracy, fidelity, and harmony of representation, in wealth and fitness of surroundings, in richness of colour, in sharpness of characteristic, and in sweetness, charm, and grace of piety. And yet they seem to have had no predecessors, no masters. We

CHRISTIANITY AND PAINTING

cannot trace the steps by which they came to be what they are.

The great representative of the German school is Albert Dürer. The realism of this school was more real and less refined than that of the Flemish School. In a crucifixion, for instance, it was fond of dwelling on the harsh features offered by the ferocity and mockery of the crowd, and too little able to make these a mere under-agent in the grand or touching effect of the scene. This intense realism gives a very special and powerful quality to Dürer's work, while he was able by his genius to overcome its disharmonies, and blend them, like the discords of Wagner, in a new, strange, and at first repellent order of art.

It would be tedious to pursue the multitude of schools and modes of representation which arose in Teutonic art (like the sects in its Protestant religion) out of its tendency to individualise, define, and secede. Yet much might be said about the Dutch and English schools. Especially as to the humour of the Dutch and its success in representing that concrete piety and burgher religion, whose breviary is in the book of Proverbs, which is so dear to the English heart, and so valuable a constituent of the world's faith. This art is nothing if not faithful and actual, but it is saved from vulgarity and grossness (where it is saved) in the one class of picture by the depth of its humour and wealth of its characterisation, in the other class by the depth, if not height, of its somewhat inarticulate piety. And as to English art, I cannot in my space say more than I have already said about landscape and the Teutonic school generally. Besides, we are now outside the region of Art expressly religious. And the subject could only be carried further by an essay on the religious element in contemporary art, a task I once tried elsewhere.[1] We might, perhaps, describe English art generally, and contemporary art in particular, as being religious rather than Christian, or, if Christian, then as working on the fringes of revelation rather than as dwelling at its source; as reading the natural face rather than the inner soul; and seeing more with the eye than in it—as science does. The methods of God show more in this art than His character. His garment is painted rather than His thought. His immanent pantheism in Manifestation shows more than his transcendent Theism in Incarnation. He is more beautiful than holy, more honoured than beloved, more regulative from without than inspiring from within us, and, at best, more the Guide and Benefactor than the Redeemer of human kind. It is not religious art nor is it anti-religious. But it is lay art. It is anti-ecclesiastical. It is free. If it serve the Christ it does so voluntarily. And it has almost given up religious subjects. It has religious sympathies and affinities more than convictions of faith.

Humanity must return within itself for the objective and authority it demands. From Nature it must again recur upon the soul, where it stood in the great pictorial age. If it is a soul we are

[1] *Religion in Recent Art.* Hodder and Stoughton.

still supremely to love, it is a soul that we must chiefly reveal in art. When the new return upon the soul has given us a more real and intimate authority there than mediævalism knew, then Humanity may return to art with new methods, new grasp, new prospect over its being's whole. It will thenceforth be inward, with a new sense of its own objective, and a new sealing of its unity with outward things. But still it must return within. The vague and pervasive quality of our present religion, its ' unconscious Christianity,' must be replaced by something more definite than itself, but also more elastic than the orthodoxy of the past, so as to give scope for the force that does really lie in the immanence that to so many is a charm. It is formidable yet intoxicating to stand on the verge of the new time, to place ourselves on the spit of land where modern thought runs farthest out into the future and unknown, to see as from a mountain the vapours of thought seething at our feet, veiling the world, and shaping themselves to nothing that for an hour endures. There is some fear but more delight in that high air. That is, if our feet are firm when the landmarks are lost. Happy is he who from such firm footing is able also to take observation of the heavens, and still to see fixed in them the ancient lights which give law to human time, and heat, life, and energy to all the earth.

VII

ARCHITECTURE, ESPECIALLY CHRISTIAN

ARCHITECTURE holds a middle place between the arts that are practical and those that are ideal, between utility and beauty. Its first purpose is to be useful. It is to satisfy a commonplace need—the need of enclosure or of shelter. It is a means, not an end in itself. It is only in its later stages that it becomes an art in the true sense of the word, an end in itself, and an expression of the soul's delight. When the needs of utility have been satisfied, it has leisure to become beautiful. When it has satisfied the practical uses of the will and of action, it turns upward to fulfil the ideal uses of emotion or of thought. The church building is first a rendezvous, a meeting-house. It is only after centuries a cathedral. Hence (speaking roughly) the first millennium of Christianity, viewed in relation to Art, is occupied entirely with architecture. No other art had any existence worth mention.

Now in Greece this was not exactly the case. Architecture was not first, and did not monopolise the artistic sphere. And why so ? Perhaps the difference between the two temples, the Greek and the Christian, may explain it. The Greek temple is meant to contain the God, in the form of his statue; the Christian temple is to contain the worshippers and not the God. He cannot be contained by any temple. The heaven of heavens cannot hold Him. He is the Infinite and Eternal. This great difference, which explains many other things, explains also the fact that architecture took the lead in Christianity as it did not in Greece. The Greek had first to make the image of his God. When that was made there arose the need of an enclosure to place it in. The Christian, on the contrary, needed no image of his God, either in wood or stone. That image was in an historic figure, real still though unseen, shrined in the Church's heart and soul. Further, Christianity, at first at least, was not an open-air religion. It was not on blithe terms with Nature. Moreover, it did not begin by being coextensive with a nation or people. Its believers had therefore to worship in gathered groups which excluded the public; and later it had to seek cover as a thing hunted by the public. All the Christian needed, therefore, was a structure to shelter himself and his fellow-worshippers, to shut them in with their devotion, and to exclude the sun, the storm, the public, and the other distracting or persecuting influences of the pagan world.

Architecture in connection with religion means, of course, the architecture of the temple. We ask, then, what is there distinctive or beautiful about the Christian temple? How far is it a work of art? How did it come to be such a work? Under what conditions did it reach its highest artistic perfection? How far does its artistic form express the religious ideas or emotions distinctive of the faith ? And how does it differ from the most perfect pagan temple, the Greek ?

The Christian temple, of course, is the cathedral (though some of the smaller churches are perhaps no less perfect in their art); and the Christian cathedral, like Rome itself, was not built in a day ; but it is the birth of a thousand moving years. It is the outcome of the whole force of an age which itself had been prepared for by nine or ten silent centuries of stored force.

For the first three centuries we have little trace of Christian edifices. The worshippers met in private houses, and in *scholæ*, lodge-rooms, or philosophic schools ; or else they shunned observation and persecution in dens and caves of the earth. They would meet also in the cella, or little apsidal chapel, built over the remains of some martyr. The young religion of Europe withdrew into upper rooms, retired to lone graves, or burrowed in catacombs ; and the new Rome thus almost literally rose from the bones and the foundations of the old. Hated by the World, suspected by the State, despised by Art, thrown, as it were, to the moles and the bats, plunged into darkness, descending into Hades, and forced to worship the divine Resurrection in the very chambers of the dead, the new faith, with its solemn germ of latent power, could have little sympathy with æsthetic beauty, and little bond with the splendid world. Death and the life unseen absorbed their thoughts. They absorbed them, but did not quench them in gloom.

The walls of those very Catacombs testify still, by their rude but sweet symbolism, the peaceful joy which overcomes the world, and which is the earnest of that later, larger, but still chastened exultation uttered in Gothic and other art. But apart from the private dwelling, the simple lodge or guild room, or the secret catacomb, there were no Christian fabrics in these early years, none designed to express Christian ideas—only for use in assembly. 'These Christians,' says Celsus, ' have neither temple nor altar.' Their very city of God itself was also thus, ' I saw no temple therein.' There was no Christian art at all. The Church had something else to do then than carve, build, paint, or poetise. They had a baptism to be baptized with, and they were straitened till it should be accomplished. They had upon their souls the task of reorganising the spiritual bankruptcy of Europe, and leavening it with their own unity of dear-bought faith and joy. And what art could grow up under the pressure of a mission, a travail, like that? It taxed even God to redeem, and the apostle of Redemption can do nothing beside. Had they had buildings for worship at that time, probably they would not have made them beautiful. But they had not. And that they had not is due, as I have suggested, to the two causes: (1) The simple spirituality of their faith, which made worship possible wherever two or three faithful souls met; (2) The opposition and persecution it met with at the hands of the Roman state. This was the time in which, as Chrysostom says, the houses were churches, the church had not yet become a house. We have, I say, the Church meeting in private houses, and then in lodges of guilds, in lecture halls, in the little memorial cellæ in the cemeteries. The church type grew out of these combined—the forecourt of the house, the oblong of the schola, the apse of the schola and cella.

But it was another matter when this strange creed, buried alive, so to speak, was exhumed, and pushed, not only into the light of day, but into the light which beats upon a throne. When Christianity was suddenly placed upon the imperial throne, for all its long entombment it took its place with no bleared vision or unsteady eye. It went straight to organise for the uses of its own spirit the forces it found in the world, and to regulate by the force of its own life the manifold resources which lay to its hand. And amongst the other furniture of the late pagan occupants, it found the basilicas, the courts of justice, which were modelled after that in the Roman forum, and were spread in every town over the Roman empire. These basilicas, rather than the pagan temples, offered affinities for the Christian Church. There was a close connection now with the imperial administration, and there was a deep and thorough hatred of the old paganism, which together explain the adoption of the basilica type and the rejection of the temple.

This, however, is to be observed. The Eastern Church developed in quite a different way from the West. The Church of the East was then more

ARCHITECTURE

liberal in its theology, as we should now say. It read Christian meanings into the pagan myths and philosophic speculations. It had not so much difficulty about using for Christian worship the temples it found in the East. The West, on the contrary, while less flexible in its theology, was very pliant in the region of practical affairs. It stepped lightly into the shoes of the great Roman administrators, and it adapted itself to the old jurisprudence, and the old imperial methods, with the same facility as the Eastern mind showed in regard to the old philosophy. We have in consequence one type of Christian building in the East, another in the West. In the East the existing temple gave the type, in the West the basilica.

A few words on the Eastern Church architecture. We are familiar with the prevalence of the dome in Eastern structures. This feature was conspicuous in the Oriental temples. But the East had been swept over by Greece, and then by Rome, and where these three met the dome was worked into the square form of structure which distinguished classic architecture. The combination was not quite harmonious, but there it is. There was one feature about the dome which commended it to Christian fancy. Rising over the centre of the building, it seemed to express the central, sublime, spacious, and comprehensive unity of God : 'over every majesty is a canopy'; while the cubical, angular, or classic structure beneath with its three dimensions seemed a symbol of the three elements of the Trinity. When, therefore, the square classic substructure was surmounted and covered by the spherical and Oriental dome, there you had, in one fabric, the symbol of the divine Trinity crowned and included by the divine unity and perfection. It is not meant that these suggestions led to the adoption of such a form. More utilitarian considerations were at work. But it became a symbolism as characteristic, though almost as accidental, in its way as that of the cross in the ground-plan of Western Gothic. The two forms were perhaps the more expressive of the genius of the two Churches because they were, in both cases, unconscious, and were rather assumed by the idea than constructed by the intention of each. You may remember that it was in the Eastern Church that the great discussions about the Trinity took place, and it is to the Eastern mind, acting under Greek influence, that we owe the theology of the Trinity. Whereas it was the Western Church that developed the theology of the Cross, of Atonement, and Redemption.

The one great specimen of this style of architecture was the Church, now the Mosque, of St. Sophia, built by Constantine in the fourth and rebuilt by Justinian in the sixth century—a marvel of splendour still—like many of those speculations to which I have referred, but in some respects also a reflection of their occasional incongruity.

The theology of the East, attractive as much of it is, liberal as much of it was for its day, became barren and worse than barren, mischievous, before long, because it lost the ethical note and retired from the practical interests of life, society, politics, and law. Liberalism is not enough to keep a church liberal. The Church strove to control these interests without pervading and inspiring them. Religion was separated from life and from positive Christian experience, and became theology only. That schism is perhaps reflected to fancy in the æsthetic incongruity and unresolved contrasts of the cube and the dome. They do not flow and melt into each other. They do not make up that organic, artistic unity which in Gothic moulds and controls the whole. And the schism had this result. As in the sphere of affairs it demoralised politics and arrested development, so in art also, in the only art they had, in church building, the type originally adopted was crystallised. There is no progress in style, and the Greek religious edifice to-day is substantially the same as the Byzantine fabric of Justinian's time. The *abuse* of theology, based on the nationalising of it, killed both politics, morality, and, of course, the most delicate of all social products—art.

To return to the West—the bold, practical, progressive West—with the world's future in its heart —the West, destined by the fusion of the political Roman, the ideal, ethical, free, and faithful Teuton, and the imaginative Kelt, to exhibit a hitherto unique combination of law, morals, thought, and beauty.

Religion, having risen from the catacomb to the throne, proceeded not only to rule but to pervade all life with the immanence of intellectual power instead of dim substance. The religious edifices, therefore, must not be used merely for the purposes of sacrifice and prayer, but also for instruction in the Christian scheme of life in all its relations, here and hereafter. Life took vaster dimensions, and became wholly religious. It demanded ritual, edification, and instruction. The religious buildings, too, must therefore expand to imperial proportions. Law and Gospel had become one, and there seemed reason now why the type of their one edifice should be found in the spacious abodes of that law and justice which, even when pagan, was recognised by Christians as divine. This was the feeling of the West; and the Western Church therefore adopted the basilica type as its meeting-place for praise, prayer, reading, homilies, and sacraments. In the light of recent research, I must not hastily say it adapted the actual basilicas.

But the basilica type had another recommendation. By the time that Christianity became the imperial religion it had come to divide men into three great classes. First there was the great world outside, the heathen—second, there was the saved, the Church—and, third, there was the élite of the elect, the holy of the holy, the clergy. It was necessary that in the house of meeting a place should be assigned for each of these. Now the pagan temple, apart from other objections, did not offer itself to such a division. The basilica did. What was the basilica like? Its original type was that in the Roman forum. It was an oblong composed of four lines of pillars supporting a roof. Sometimes the pillars were enclosed with a wall.

ARCHITECTURE

At one end was a vestibule like the forecourt of the Roman house. At the other was a circular recess like the apse of the schola or cella, and there was a large pillared space between. In the recess was the judge's tribunal. In the large middle space was the public involved in the business. In the vestibule were the comers and goers and loungers. What could lend itself more readily to the Christian classification of mankind ? There in the circular apse the clergy could sit. There in the central hall the great mass of Christians could congregate. There in the vestibule might stand the curious of the world, or the catechumens, or the penitents—who were not yet ready for the interior society of the saved. The basilica type, therefore, was adopted ; and the relative proportions of these three parts went on changing as the relations and proportions changed of the different classes to each other. At first what was a mere vestibule in the Roman basilica was, in the Christian, expanded into quite a large forecourt for the learners, the penitents, or the worldly. But soon the world became the Church. The empire became Christian, and every member of it tended to be held a Christian by right of birth and baptism. It was inevitable, therefore, that the forecourt should vanish. It fell down to a mere porch, and the pillars in front of it then became the front pillars of the main building. But as the line between Church and the world faded, that between clergy and people was more firmly traced. The clergy grew both in numbers and importance. The apse soon became too small to contain them. They overflowed into the space just in front of the apse, where at first the communion table, and then the altar, was. There they formed the choir, especially where the new basilica was built against the cella of a martyr. Then the basilican apse joined with the cella to deepen the recess, as in the Gothic choir. Still they grew, but now, instead of coming forward and ousting the laity in the nave, they expanded laterally. A wing was thrown out on each side of the altar. That wing is now called the transept, and it arose for the accommodation of the growing clergy. In the end the choir was first separated, and then raised both in floor and ceiling. The pillars also were increased to diminish the sense of width and increase the height; and then the choir was decorated. At last you have the final ground-plan of the Christian Church, preserved ever afterwards amid many modifications and extensions,— the shape of the Cross. The utilities of Christian worship precipitate themselves by the providence of need in the form of a cross; and the Christian building becomes, with unconscious significance, the reflection of the central Christian idea. This ground-plan was not consciously adopted because it was the Christian symbol. It is the unconscious form which the utilities and successive exigencies of worship required. The symbolism was originally a product of utility and not of any idealism or art, however simple and rude. The cathedral in its main form, then, is simply a schola or lodge room developed through the cella and basilica. The modification was due partly to its environment,

ARCHITECTURE

partly to the needs and genius of the Christian spirit, whose earthly garment and tabernacle it was. And the fine fabric of the Gospel is, in part at least, a development of the older structure of the law.

With few exceptions all the churches of the West were built in this basilica style from about 300 to 1000 A.D. It was, in art, as in many other things, an unprogressive age. Christianity was still struggling with some pagan influences and absorbing others, classic or barbarian. It was at the same time preparing to leaven Europe more deeply than ever before with a new force. That leaven was silent, secret, and subterranean—repeating in a figure the first contact of Christianity and Empire. The machinery and dress of the faith was like the church building, classical. And it was of a mixed classic sort. The Christian spirit was unable quite to assimilate the pagan forms it was forced to use. Nor could it fuse with its heat the old varieties into a new unity. These were slow centuries, when the Christian spirit was acquiring an individuality of its own, which in due course would express itself in an art of its own. The Teutonic peoples, the Romance and Keltic peoples, and the Classical peoples were all like a Ravenna mosaic as yet. They were composite, but not yet fused into a new substance with a spirit and quality of its own. Christian art, therefore, like the Christian empire, was heterogeneous, a medley, an amalgam. The pure simplicity of classic art was spoiled, and a new art inspiration was not yet to hand. So, in the tenth century we have still, in various degrees of rich and even barbaric adornment, the Roman basilica as the typical church, the decoration being almost all spent on the interior, and the outside left very plain and bare. That is the first period of Christian architecture, the Roman or basilica period, the period of the Dark Ages, say from A.D. 300 to A.D. 1000 roughly.

The second period is from 1000 to 1200. Its name is often given as the Romanesque period. It shows a decided advance, and stands as a sort of vestibule to the great Gothic structures which were immediately to rise. I said the ground-plan and typical form of the church was fixed comparatively early—the form of the Cross. The changes that now take place are in the style, not in the plan. What is the mark of this period, then? It is to be found in the arch. In the Roman basilica the square Greek style of pillar and beam was united with the round Roman arch, and the two exist side by side, neither subduing the other, like the theology and ethics in the Church itself. The roof of the church, *e.g.*, had been composed of beams, which were supported by the pillars and walls. But about 1000 A.D. the specially Roman feature of the arched vault took the lead. The beams were abolished, and the roof took a circular form, bearing upon the side walls of the fabric. We begin to see now that groined and vaulted roof which is so indispensable to Gothic art. One element has become supreme. Rome has got the

ARCHITECTURE

upper hand of Greece, the West of the East, the arch of the beam. Ascendency gives more prospect of unity, and therefore more hope for Art. Another unity appears in material as well as style. Wood vanishes and stone is used throughout. The very pillar vanishes to some extent, and the round Roman arch, starting from the ground, or from a low pillar, occupies with its unity of curve the place before filled by the right angle with its two lines of pillar and beam. The exterior of the building begins to receive more attention, and a tower begins to rise over the centre of the cross. This is what is known (though not unanimously) as the Romanesque style. It displays the presence of new elements, and especially a new tendency to unity as expressed in the arch, to aspiration as expressed in the tower and the vault, and to beauty as expressed in the decoration of the outside. The Christian spirit was slowly beginning to make its æsthetic individuality felt. The Keltic and Teutonic peoples were beginning to contribute their part. Here we have, then, the germinal expression in art of Roman unity or power, Teutonic aspiration or idealism, and Keltic beauty or charm. It remained only to develop these and perfectly fuse them.

But the greatest step was yet to be taken. The arched vault had a further development to receive; and it came concurrently with the splendid outbreak of artistic, civil, and other freedom about the thirteenth century. At one step the circular arch passed into the pointed arch, and with this the pent soul received a tongue. Where the pointed arch came from is not quite clear—some say from the Saracens, through the Crusades. Perhaps it was but an utilitarian discovery as giving greater strength than the arch. But it was Europe, not the East that knew how to use it—the Christian, not the Moslem, spirit. This change, simple and grand, furnished an organ for an outburst of conjoined piety and genius paralleled only by the Reformation. The classic disappeared before the Gothic, which rose probably in northern France, and spread quickly over northern Europe. The South felt now in Art the powerful and renovating influence of that northern spirit, faithful and free, which centuries before had morally reinvigorated the worn-out empire. The North, lay, liberal, and true, reanimates the clerical South. The realism of the North assumes in architecture this ideal quality which was in the South reserved for painting alone.

The round arch is heavy and lowering. It is weak in the middle; and it bears upon the side walls with a thrust which necessitates their being made very thick and strong. This further adds to the heavy effect, especially as the windows must be small lest the bearing power of the wall be impaired. This defect was especially felt when the arch, as often happened, was less than a semicircle. The lateral thrust was then very great. It was impossible with this circular form of arch, and its heavy, though solid, suggestions, either to express Christian aspiration, or exhibit the grace of spiritual beauty. It was therefore a splendid stroke to replace the single curve, described from one centre, by a pair of curves bearing upon each other, and drawn from different centres in the same straight line of base. It was a stroke comparable, for its effect in art, with the invention of movable type in literature, or the cipher in arithmetic. And it developed with a rapidity and fertility which showed that it was the one thing needful in this kind to release the artistic spirit of the time. All that makes the beauty and special glory of the Gothic cathedral or chapel lies latent in the simple beauty and utility of that leaf-like pointed arch. Aspiration received a fitting symbol. It is like two hands joined in tense perpetual prayer. Lightness and grace became now first possible. The great strength of this arch reduced the necessity for massive walls, few windows, and large unbroken surfaces. The whole support of the roof could now be relegated to the pillars from which the pointed arch sprang. The wall space between them could be broken up into windows, which again reproduced in small the structural grace of the whole. The church rose, as it were, in the scale of organised life. From a crustacean it became a vertebrate. Instead of a case or shell, it got a skeleton. It became sinewy rather than massive, lithe instead of gross. Like the constitution of the hierarchy itself, the burden of supporting the fabric of the church was removed from the masses and laid upon a few strong, refined, and lofty shoulders. A new field was also given for decorative art. The parts, like the window spaces, which had been released from the function of support could now be devoted to the purposes of beauty. Just as a man or a nation that has established by toil and conflict a position in the world, and delegated to others the conduct of business and the support of mere life, may turn with free and ready mind to the culture of beauty or the fascination of thought.

This, then, was the culmination of Christian architecture, the Romantic style, called best the pointed style, and, less happily, the French or German, or Teutonic style, and worst of all the Gothic. I need hardly remind you that in the eighteenth century this art was considered barbarous, and many of its great monuments left unfinished, or used for stables or magazines; and it was accordingly designated by the word Gothic, which then meant what Vandalistic would mean now. Its date is from 1200 to 1400 A.D. That is the period which saw the inception of all those Gothic cathedrals and chapels which are the glory of the lands that possess them. The style is the purest, most adequate, and most congenial expression of the Christian spirit in architecture. All the styles which have followed it have been mixtures or imitations either of itself or of pagan and classic art, and, however imposing or useful, they are less expressive. They sank through the Renaissance style to the Rococo of the Jesuit churches abroad, with their whitewashed walls and carved wood, reminding us of the later era of horsehair sofas and wax flowers in the window. Whatever the future may have in store, no independent style of Christian architecture has since that Gothic

ARCHITECTURE

age appeared. And we are safe to say that probably none will appear, till, if ever, Christianity and Christendom regain on a vaster scale the unity which alone made the cathedrals possible. They drew upon the whole resources of a unified age; their marvellous unity of structure expressed it; and they made the draft at a moment when the unity of the Western Church was conterminous with the unity of the civilised world, and in command of its best energies. But when the Reformation came, it found Christendom well supplied with churches. And, ever since, its Christianity has been, on the one hand, too spiritual and inward—like the first three centuries, or else, on the other, too confused and divided to care for a great plastic art, or to make it possible if it did care. (The case is different in regard to music.) Or like the early centuries it has been too engrossed with the reconquest of Europe, the conversion of Christendom from its paganism, the treatment of the new economic situation, the solution of its political and social problems, to have spiritual leisure for a distinctive art. The great new movement at first tended, either in the white renaissance of culture, or the black renaissance in Calvinism, to precise and rational form, which, exalted by the abundance of revelation, had little affinity for the mediæval chiaroscuro and the too dim mysteries of faith.

It is true that there is a sense in which Christianity is not favourable to Art. Its moral genius forefeels in it a worldly foe. Its individualism is sometimes excessive and narrow. Its sects lose touch of the real motive of the age. But over and above all that is its spiritual stability and security. It can, from the height of its spiritual exaltation, too easily dispense with Art. Its supreme joy is unspeakable and full of mystic glory. In the communion of the soul with God, both Nature and Art are forgotten, and the media of outward expression are not required.

> Theirs is the language of the heavens, the power,
> The thought, the image, and the silent joy.
> Words are but under-agents in their souls;
> When they are grasping with their greatest strength
> They do not breathe among them. In such hour
> Of visitation from the most high God
> Thought is not, in emotion it expires.

This Middle Age was the age of great structures and subtle fabrics. It is an old popular delusion that the European mind was in its infancy till the pagan Renaissance and the Reformation. But one of the feats of the nineteenth century was to discover the thirteenth. The fact is, there has never been in Europe an age in which the human mind worked with nobler ambitions, or more harmonious and joyful ease, than the age of which I now speak. In every region of the soul it was a great structural period. In the region of the will, of government, it was the age of that mighty fabric the Holy Roman Empire. In the region of thought, it was the age of that great and fine fabric the scholastic philosophy and theology. In the region of the feelings it was the age in which devotion and genius reared the lovely structure of the Gothic cathedral.

ARCHITECTURE

In the region of poetry it was Dante's age. And in that of painting it was the age of the masters of early Italian and Flemish art. It was the age in which, by a mighty effort of the soul, man sought to bring all things earthly under a visible unity reflecting the central and organising unity of the Universe. It had the cosmic, the architectonic, note, as far as its cosmos went. Human affairs were to be unified by the power of the sacred empire. Matters of thought were to own the total sway of one system, whose very ruins to-day are tremendous. And all the resources of Art were to be subjected to that unity of spiritual beauty, which co-ordinates the vast variety of cathedral decoration and structure.

What now were the features of that Gothic art as expressed in the Christian temple, especially in contrast with the pagan temple of Greece?

1. This art sprang not from the clergy, but from the laity. The great master builders were not among the priests, but among the people. And here we remember in passing that this was also the age of the birth of civil or municipal freedom. These builders are for the most part quite unknown. We know the man whose genius informed the political fabric of the Holy Roman Empire: it was Gregory the Seventh. We know the great master of its intellectual fabric of scholastic thought: it was Thomas Aquinas. Priests both. We know who gathered the whole age together in an imaginative world ranging from hell to heaven: it was Dante. But we do not know who first saw, or

who chiefly developed, the resources of the pointed arch, and made them the beautiful garment of Christian piety and praise. We only know that its master builders were laymen, and that to the last the Church in its headquarters of Italy was chary of recognising their work of revolution and advance. Speaking generally, we do not get Gothic churches south of Milan.

2. The next feature of this art is its inwardness. The plan of the building converges towards one point in the interior—the centre of the cross. And the structure of the walls from their straight ascent curve inward to meet overhead, as if to enclose the worshipper with Deity, and to symbolise in its hour of prayer the ascending but humbled and concentrated soul. The low doors are sunk into the thick wall, and the masonry contracts as it approaches them; as if to indicate how the outward must bow, dwindle, and vanish as the inward sanctuary of the soul is approached. It is in the inside that the serious business of worship is transacted, and many a device like the staining of the window glass is used to deaden the impact of the gay, bold, outward world.

It was otherwise in the Greek temple. There the mass of the people were outside in the garish day, and it was consequently the outside of the small building that received most of the artist's attention. The central cell with the statue of the god was in some cases never entered by man. The temple, therefore, as it was the garment of the god, not of the worshippers, had its seamy side inmost. Its beauty was turned upon the world without, which was more to the Greek than his god, after all. Man throughout this religion was more than God, and though the god was sheltered, it was the man that was delighted. There is besides no convergence here towards a central point. The pillars are outside, not inside the wall. They form only a limit, not an enclosure. And the central shrine was in many cases, like the Greek mind, open at the top to all the natural influences of sun, wind, and world. The tendency throughout in the Greek temple was centrifugal, not centripetal, and the suggestions were those of worship dispersed rather than concentrated, a blithe pantheism rather than a solemn theism. It was a light, volatile, and often idle people that congregated in busy groups about the pillars and steps of the Greek temple. They were outside the seriousness of life. The vastness of the cathedrals, compared with the classic temple, points the same way. They were built to hold a whole local community inside, and to give space for the performance of a variety of sacred functions at once. So we may say that while Greek religion in its architecture illuminated the stone from without, Christian religion shone through it and transfigured it from within.

3. The next feature is the chastened sadness of this art. The daylight is broken and tempered. It is in the light of another than the earthly day that the worshipper for the time lives. There is a droop in the arches which meet and mingle around and over him, as if the soul went upwards under a heavy load of sorrow and sin, and the righteous

scarcely were saved. We have not here the joy of intellectual knowledge, the delight of a free and careless imagination, as in Greece. It is the power of sorrowful, reverent faith, not the clear vision of the rational soul. God and the world were reconciled, to be sure, but the reconciliation was believed in rather than clearly worked out in its steps and method, or grasped in the fulness of its victory. It is just in this age, we should remember, with Anselm, that the speculations about the nature of the reconciling act, as distinct from its mere fact, really begin; and the elements of the great and tragic problem were less clear than they are now. It was through an atmosphere clouded and laden, a social atmosphere of sin, violence, and ignorance, from which many of the fine spirits escaped into monasteries, that the soul went up to God. It went up sadly but hopefully, bowed but persistent, faint yet pursuing. That and more is in the dim, bowed, mysterious sadness of the interior of the Gothic church. There is none of it in the square, self-contained, and sprightly temple of Greece.

4. This quality of sadness sprang from what is perhaps the leading feature of Gothic art—its aspiration. It is the utterance of a quickened and bursting age. It is hard to realise the effect on the human soul of the idea of infinity which Christianity inserted and naturalised into human life. It turned life from content to aspiration, and troubled the joy of quiescence with the tremulous excitement of a high dissatisfaction and an endless hope. That eternal hope and aspiration speaks forth in

every line and curve of the Gothic architecture, especially in its exterior, where the sense of inwardness has not to be realised. It is the lovely symbol of man's thirst for the infinite. It is 'thrust like a fine question heavenward.' It utters man's dissatisfaction with himself, and expresses his rest and peace to be only in God.

> Splendour, proof,
> I keep the brood of stars aloof,
> For I intend to get to God.[1]

It is the soul of the *Imitation* projected in stone. The pointed arch, reproduced in great and small throughout the whole fabric, the upright line instead of the classic horizontal, the vast height of the pillars prolonged into the roof, the effect produced by bundles of small pillars rolled into one column, and carrying the eye upward along their small light shafts, the judicious use of external carving, so as to add to the effect of height instead of reducing it, the pinnacles and finials which run up everywhere on the outside, the tower, and still more the spire, placed above all these—the total effect was to make the spirit travel upwards with the eye and lose itself in the infinity of space. The whole building seems chained to earth in fixed flight. I have seen Lincoln Cathedral from miles to the west like a great eagle cowering with spread wings just in the act of taking flight. The cathedral is a lyric sigh and a carved prayer. The lightness of the structure, its ethereal fineness, seems to spurn a nest on earth. *Spernit humum fugiente*

---
[1] Browning: Johannes Agricola in Meditation.

penna. It rises like an exhalation from the soil. The fabric seems almost organic and tremulous with life. No architecture like the Gothic so spiritualises, refines, and casts heavenward the substance which it handles. It volatilises the stone. It gives the garment of praise for the spirit of heaviness.

Compare the Greek temple. It was broad, not high. The eye travels not up, but along. It satisfies rather than inspires. It is stable, not aspiring. It cleaveth to the dust; or, if that be too strong an expression for art so perfect in its way, it sits well throned and says, I shall be a lady for ever in my own right and grace. It looks neither down nor up. It is based, like the religion, on the solid ground of Nature. It is far from squat, but it is not lofty. It is, compared with the ladyhood of Gothic, but a four-footed thing, the gracefullest of them all, an antelope, or, to use a figure more congenial to Greece, a noble horse, but not

> A woman yet, not bright
> With something of angelic light.[1]

5. The next feature is its beauty, and that not so much now in its gracefulness as in its richness. The passion of divine love with which Christianity enriched mankind, as it were pours itself out here in an exuberance of decoration, held in check, at the best period of the art, only by the grand unity and central simplicity of the whole. Never before was such a wealth of beauty poured into fabric. The churches of the East and the basilicas of the West had been laden with metals, with colours and

---

[1] Wordsworth: "She was a phantom of delight" (adapted).

other foreign ornaments, and it was all inside. The kings of the earth brought their glory and honour into it; but they were Oriental kings with barbaric colour, pearl and gold. But here matter itself is transfigured. The stone itself is quickened and beautified. It is the form that is carved into eloquence; it is no other art that is called in to atone for architectural impotence. And the outside is even richer than within. Part of the purpose of this was to increase the effect of height. For it is now well known that carving if judiciously used does so; while if it is not used at all, or if it is lavished, the effect is reversed, the height of the structure appears to the eye reduced. But this was only partly the reason of so much embellishment. It satisfied as well the desire of the pious builder of that day to expand the wealth of his heart and the richness of his genius in the service of Christ and His Church. And, beyond that, it expressed the vast variety which the unity of the Church strove to comprehend and work up into her own estate. Nor are we going too far in viewing the cathedral as a miniature creation, and as representing the vast variety of creation, even to its grotesquerie, held together by the immanence and transcendence of the divine, subtle, and manifold spirit.

It would be easy, of course, to fall into fanciful symbolism in a case like this, and I will go no further. But now contrast the Greek temple. The Greek temple was very sparing in decoration. Its idea was simple, and much carving would impair it. Its size was not great, and excessive decoration would reduce it. It had just as much ornament as made it seem its right size. It abounded in long lines and flat surfaces. And the artist had not the Christian Franciscan passion of love, burning in his heart, overflowing his genius, and breaking into a thousand scattered lights as it fell upon his work.

6. The next feature is that of unity. As the whole was grouped about one form of the Cross, so the whole was pervaded by one thought and one emotion. It was throughout Catholic in its suggestion and its tendency. It was only in its later and less perfect stages that the decoration became too florid, and submerged this unity and simplicity, as the Middle Age altogether died of its subtleties, especially in its dialectic. In its best years the ornament was held in vigorous subordination by the pervasive spirit. The fancy was ruled by the imagination. The organising thought was not lost in detail, or scattered into fragments. The organic unity of true art pervaded and braced the whole. It made the edifice one fabric. As religion governs all the energies of the soul, as all lives are embraced in the Divine Life, as the kingdom of God (represented by the Catholic Church) governed by right all the kingdoms of men, as the spirit of the Creator in the universe governs the whole infinity and multiplicity of created detail, so the spirit of Christian worship, the greatest act of which creation is capable, included harmoniously all the elaboration and variety of detail in Gothic art. The grand lines of the structure shone out through it all, and overruled it. And the great Christian idea of sacrifice was by this expressed. Every part was willingly

subservient and devoted to the whole and therefore to God. The statues were not stuck on the buildings, but each had its organic place, and the niches were as the many mansions of the Father's house. The individual sculptures, like the individual man, must bow to the Church as the vicegerent of God and find their own true place in doing so. And thus was embodied the communion of saints, the communion of sacrifice, of the Cross, the communion of a redeemed world, where we are all members one of another, and of the new Humanity as the body of Christ.

And this effect is enhanced by considering the unity between the outside and inside of the building, as it were between the life of aspiration in the world, and that of inward devotion in the Church. The external aspect of the building corresponds to the inward arrangement. A window outside is one inside also. The features of nave, aisle, transept, chancel, seen from without are also found within. This unity did not exist in the Greek temples. There the outside, as already said, was very different from the inside, and gave no idea of what the inside was like. The soul and the world were not yet quite reconciled. The outer and the inner man were not quite at peace.

The concinnity of the cathedral, its organic solidarity, secured not by accumulated weight but by the perfect equilibrium of forces and unity of antagonisms, its resemblance thus to the frame of Nature, and to the spiritual church or human society—all this offers a literal example of Paul's words, 'in whom the whole building fitly framed together, and perfected by that which every joint supplieth, groweth into an holy temple in the Lord.'

7. This unity produces the effect of peace. But the peace of Christianity is very different from the calm of Greece. The peace in Christianity is the solemn calm of intense movement, of progress, of upward life, of unresting development and aspiration for the unworldly but assured. It is certainty and confidence. It is Sabbatic—the rest of the Creator, whose might upheld creation even in His rest. It is expressed in the spring of the Gothic arch, and the noble flight of the whole fabric. The roof is apparently less supported by the pillars than springing from them, less a load than a product, as a branch from a tree, less a burden than a new facility, like wheels on the chariot, or like wings upon the bird. The calm of Greece, on the contrary, was the calm of repose, of resignation, of a condition of static finality, not of development or aspiration, not the dynamic finality of Christianity. The ancient world altogether was unfamiliar with the idea of progress, because it had not the powerful repose of faith. It was the stoic calm of endurance, bearing up, with self-centred force, according to Nature's law, against the vicissitudes of fate and life. And that is the calm which is typified in the architecture of the pillar and beam, the supporting and supported, which is the structure of the Greek temple. It is the idea of resistance to downward pressure, bearing on shoulders Atlantean the too vast orb of its fate; it is not the idea of a leap in a kindred element, 'an upward springing blithe to

ARCHITECTURE

greet the purpling morn,' not the heavenly elasticity which glories in tribulations, and thrives on adversity, and if sorrowful is always rejoicing in hope of the glory of God. Above the one is fate, above the other is God.

8. If Christianity were an æsthetic religion, the Gothic cathedral would be its finished and perpetual type, the fit garment of a worship the most imaginative and beautiful the world knows. Impressive and significant ritual can go no further than the Mass; and the Mass could not be more fitly housed than in the cathedral, which cries out for a worship not merely ornate, but truly poetic and splendid. In such a fabric a simple service seems bald, and affects us as if the clergyman officiated in a jacket. The cathedral is the shrine of a spectacular worship, which appeals to the seeing of the eye rather than the hearing of the ear. It is constructed for ceremonies and processions. Æsthetics rule all. Acoustics are disregarded. More is not required than that the fabric should re-echo an intoned service or the holy murmur of the Mass, and allow vision to participators who are chiefly spectators of a magical act done by one of the worshipping order. They are rather within its sphere of influence than within the communion of the act.

But Christianity is not an æsthetic religion, it is an ethical. At the centre of its worship is not a magical act of God but a moral, in whose nature every Christian must share with an active partnership, and not a passive presence. Its worship centres in an active Saviour who is more than a godly spectacle. The death of Christ was God's supreme moral act; and it is presented to the world by something which is *ejusdem generis*, in so far as that it also is an act. Ritually it is expressed in a communion and not a Mass; in a communion shared, and not a sacrifice offered; in a communion act in which all who form the Church equally partake, and not in a ceremony where the real actors are but the few. And outside the ritual sphere divine service is the utterance of an intelligible Word, which reflects the intelligibility of the Cross as experienced by the conscience, and not merely the credited mystery of a God who became incarnate by any such process as transubstantiation can express. It is the Word of a moral miracle, and not a material, however fine and spiritualised. It is a worship wherein all are priests, and all co-agents in the utterance of the Word to the rational conscience, the personal experience, and the moral imagination.

To this conception of Christianity the Christian building should correspond. And it seals the fate of the Gothic style. For the purposes of an evangelical Christianity, where everything turns on a preached Gospel and vernacular prayer, that style is quite inadequate. It is not beauty we want in the fabric, as it is not splendour it is meant to house. The first consideration is acoustical, and it is one less ignored by the Gothic architects than precluded by the Gothic style. The intelligible word is lost in those long aisles and lofty vaults. A vivacious critic once said it was the devil that invented Gothic to prevent the people from hearing the Gospel. Allowing for the mythology, the remark is not absurd. As Christianity grows more ethically spiritual, it must become more impatient, for its present uses, of a style which corresponds but to one type of it, where the spiritual imagination ousts the quickened conscience. The æsthetic type will never lose its beauty, and it has much to teach those forms of Christianity where the moral too easily sinks to the bald, trivial, and humdrum. But the ruling type of such a religion as that of the New Testament must be revelation, and not mystery, and its vehicle must be the spoken word, which in its truth and purity is a great *act* of appeal to the intelligent will of God or man. And while there is much in some modern church fabrics that may suggest a religious factory or a philanthropic industry, yet that is only an exaggeration of one side of a true and effective Gospel as the Roman worship is the hypertrophy of another side, which is but a side after all. The church must be primarily an auditorium, even when it is not preaching but prayer that we have in view. And the style of building now, as at the first, must develop according to that practical purpose, and not according to an æsthetic ideal. The contemplative, speculative nature of the Catholic ideal is reflected in its æsthetic fabric; the practical nature, the moral, the intelligible, nature of the evangelical ideal must give the type of a fabric instinct with purpose rather than charm. For it must serve the uses of a Gospel of God's purpose with the world, and a kingdom which is not identical with the Church, but is pursued by the Church as its agent or preluded by it as its dawn.

VIII

MUSIC

WE pass now into a new region, and reach the domain of a new sense. Hitherto we have walked by the seeing of the eye, now we must live by the hearing of the ear. The arts of sight are manifold. The art of hearing is but one. Architecture, sculpture, painting all depend on the eye. Music alone lives for the ear. Those others lead us about in a world that is still outward to ourselves. This plunges us into our own soul's depths, explores with us the winding ways of passion, and wakes us to the knowledge of a whole vibrant world within, of brimming tides and rushing streams, of wild heights and misty deeps, of elemental tumult and of peace unspeakable, however brief. Brief it may be, but it cannot be spoken, and it must be sung. We wail, or sob, or shout for joy; we despair, we yearn, we exult; we are conscious of thoughts which lie too deep for tears, we hold tremendous colloquies, we expatiate, far from dumbly, in a speechless world; we learn that when words are ended the half has not been told, and that there is that within us which we cannot utter to man or woman born, but can only pour it forth, in this universal language of the soul, into the

MUSIC

bosom of the spirit that moves unheard, but not unfelt, through all things. Under the spell of music we live a history whose stir is unheard by our nearest; and we utter a praise which does not issue by our lips, but passes pure and undisturbed into the audience of the ever-open ear. Unspoken epics, unacted tragedies, lyrics that will never scan, transpire within us. And it is all within. If they escape it is, as it were, by the skylights. They pass out by none of the ordinary channels of the soul. They do not issue by the common door. They do not mingle with the crowd in the street. They go, silently and unbeheld, into the upper presence and brooding silence of God.

In a previous lecture[1] I thought we could arrange the arts according to their material elements in what I called a scale of progressive attenuation of ascending refinement, or spiritualisation. And I pointed out that this arrangement corresponded in the main to their order of historical development, and also to that of their spiritual inwardness. We had, first, the symbolic arts, represented by architecture, where the material was heavy and gross, where the forms were geometrical, inorganic, and where there was offered but a hull or tenement for the spirit, and nothing which shaped itself exactly to its form. The Gothic we saw wondrously transcended those gross conditions, and came nearer than any other architecture to being a real expression of the spirit instead of a mere garment for it. Then we had the classic art of sculpture, where the spirit took not a garment merely but a body, which

[1] p. 106.

it made perfectly instinct with its own life so far as it had then developed. Here the form was an organic, and not a merely mechanical one. But still the material was heavy. It was stone. And it stood out in a somewhat obvious and unspiritual way. The material element was too forward still. The suggestions were not inward enough. It was an outward, earthly, natural life which was cast into this splendid mould. You did not feel by looking at the statue that there was a vast spiritual Hinterland to the Greek soul, waiting and longing for some artist to loose it and let it go. All that soul was there in that stone form. No pathetic, spiritual inadequacy looked forth in yearning from those marble eyes. Your thought was detained on this perfection, and not transmitted, not cast onward to another world. Then we had the specially Romantic or Christian art of painting, where we did pass inward, and thread some of the subtler, more sacred passages of the soul. We found that in painting the material suddenly fined away from stone to light and colour. We found in consequence a quite new power of uttering the inward and spiritual. The material was light, not heavy as in architecture. It could flow subtly into individual characters, instead of dealing with types of beauty merely, as sculpture did. It could utter the heart and not the mind alone. The effect indeed was hardly produced by anything worth calling a material at all. Still, though the three dimensions of sculpture had been reduced to the flat alone, space was involved. There was a distinct outwardness. Though the picture was a liquid mirror and melting reflection of reality, yet it was also a tangible reality itself. You could put your finger on it, and even through it. And it had a distinct and permanent existence. It was there, on the wall, in its frame, when you had gone away. It was a corporeal thing.

The romantic, inward, spiritual element in Art had at least one other step to make. It had to be stripped of this outwardness, this corporeal existence. It had to win an existence which was only in the human soul itself. It had to cast off from the work of art all dealings with space, even the film of the picture's surface, and employ only the effects of time and tone. And then Art appeared as Music —the youngest, and most inward, and spiritual, of all the arts.

The picture, I say, is there when you leave it— on the wall; and there you find it when you come back. It resists your finger. A boy could put a hole in it with a stone, a knave ruin it with a knife. But where is the sonata when you have left the piano, the fugue when you have left the church? In whose power is it to deform or ruin that artistic unity and structure? It is not on the music sheets. They are but as the print is to poetry. They contain but a sort of mnemonic help to the player, and many a player does not require them. There is no art in their production. Nor is it in the strings, or in the pipes. The art which placed *them* there is very slight, and if you spoil one you can get another. At the dead of night when player and audience are alike unconscious, when the pages are locked up, and the pipes are still, while the painting is hanging in its permanent beauty on the wall, where is the work of musical art?

Let us ask a greater question to answer that. The mighty harmony of Nature and movement of history, the order which is visible in the heavens and audible in the huge city's hum, had once a beginning, and it will one day have an end. Where was it before it took this outward beginning? Where will it be when all comes to its end? The only answer to this question will to some be but little of an answer. It was, and it will be for ever, in the Eternal Mind and Soul. A day will come when the painting will fade, when the colours will crack off, and the precipitate of the mightiest genius will fall in dull flakes and mean dust on the floors. Where then will be that work of Art? Treasured, first, to a life beyond life in the eternal structure of those spirits that drank in its beauty, and absorbed its thought into their own being; and stored, next, in that Eternal and Infinite Soul, to whom a thing of beauty is indeed a possession and a joy for ever, and who forgets no work of hope or labour of love. The books of poetry will be burned up when we fall into the sun, but the poem like the soul is a spiritual shape, made of the true asbestos which God made and not man, nay, which God is made of, and not to be scorched even by a furnace which melts the elements of nature to chaos again. As, then, on the vast historic scale, time vibrates and passes away into Eternity, having moulded human spirits to dwell with the Infinite One, so, on the small scale, the organised surges of a symphony rise from the Eternal through the shaping spirit of imagination, emerge upon our consciousness, and then hastily pass into the Eternal again; taking with them, however, some portion of man's labour, love and power to store and fund on our behalf in the invisible world. It is in a Spirit, in a human or a divine consciousness, that a work of musical art really exists. It is a spiritual and inward form. It has no permanent outward existence. It does not exist apart from the listening spirit. We found that the statue was very independent of the spectator's sympathy; while the picture, by demanding a particular view point, took him into confidence, and made him, as it were, part of its own artistic unity. But in music, the listening, sympathetic spirit is still more indispensable, still more closely bound up with the artist and his work. And hence it is that nobody has so much enjoyment of musical art as the musician himself. He has in himself an audience in complete sympathy and intimate relation with the productive spirit; and the intermediate agency of the material element is reduced to the very lowest point.

In music, then, the material and corporeal all but vanishes. The string becomes musical only as it becomes invisible in its vibrations. It ' passes trembling in music out of sight.' And it is a similar vibration, a motion tending towards invisibility, which is the basis of musical sound in the trumpet, the organ pipe, or even the drum. It could almost seem as if this sensitive relation between music and moving matter were indicated in those old fables, how

> Orpheus with his lute made trees,
> And the mountain tops that freeze
> Bow themselves when he did sing;[1]

and how Amphion reared the walls of Thebes with stones that leaped to his lute; and how the spheres that roll and vibrate in the sky utter a music far too fine for sensual ears. There is no deeper mystery than this, that a trembling string should touch the very soul, that vibrations which are calculable as so many hundred taps per second on the auditory nerve should rouse or melt the whole spirit and nature of men, crowds, and nations in a way that is remembered and felt anew for ever, a way that has no inconsiderable effect in shaping both our inmost life and our public history. And how better can you explain it than by the faith that it is a divine Orpheus at work, whose energy is inherent music, who casts all matter into these tremors of delight, and who sends his spirit along the sensuous wire in fine surges to a spirit at the human end. There is melody at each end of the vibration because there is a spirit at each end. Beasts and idiots do not own the sway of music; it even exasperates them, because it is mere vibration or irritation untransfigured by the soul which has not emerged, or has retired. It is powerless where there is no soul. It would be powerless were there but one soul in the universe. It is powerful because there are two souls at the least. If there

[1] Henry VIII, III, I.

is music in man, it is because there is music in God. And in the praise we sing we return with interest but what He gave, and His Word does not return to Him void. May we not go on to say that the tumult of life is but the vibration which makes in heaven a note, and that the tremors of the earth, even its catastrophes, are at the far end music and praise?

This fugitive and momentary existence of the material element, then, gives a conspicuous inwardness to music. When the visibility of the picture passes into the audibility of music, we call into play a sense more spiritual than sight, and one which better suits the recipient and often passive attitude of the soul in the hour of spiritual revelation. There are no muscles to the ear as there are muscles we call into play for the use of the eye. We have no sense of effort. We simply receive. And we receive almost the very emotion itself; so slight is the part played by the merely material element in the sound. Music is the most sacramental, or at least the most absolute, of arts, for the elements sink to a film, and the communion is all in all.

I have previously described this inwardness as one of the chief marks of the Romantic Arts, *i.e.* those which rose to their maturity under Christian and spiritual influence, and which, even in their secularised forms, exhibit, deep in their structure, this original type and note. I am tempted, therefore, to dwell on another aspect of this inwardness and spirituality in music—that being, as I say, the art which exhibits it most. I mean its *unpictorial* quality. It exhibits it more than poetry does in one respect at least. The vocal sound in poetry is only a small part of the art. Poetry can dispense with the music of words. For Browning was a great poet who had not much of that gift. The sounds, the words, are in poetry but symbols of thoughts, or images. They please by what they suggest, they are not an end and a delight in themselves. But in music the sounds are such an end. In poetry they are but a means. A means for what ? To convey certain thoughts or images ; and it is this thought or imagery that produces the chief part of the poetic effect. In poetry, by means of sound, *i.e.* by words (which were spoken before they were written), a picture is placed before the mind, however swiftly or subconsciously, and it is the presence of this that has the artistic effect. A mental picture, then, however unconsciously, however briefly, intervenes between the sound and the emotion in poetry. The material, the formal, which we thought we had left entirely behind, with its last refinement in painting, comes back under the still more refined forms of the imagination; and the emotion is raised by a kind of subjective picture gallery, or chamber of imagery, through which in a poem we are led. But there is no intervention of imagery or picture, even of this refined and imaginative sort, in music. There is no sensuous image raised to produce the effect. Like religion often, it shrinks from sensuous imagery, even as recalled by memory or imagination. The moving power lies in the revealing mystery of sound itself and its collocations. It is, so to speak, a revelation by the Word itself, not by our thoughts about the Word, or our conception of it. It is another link between music and Christianity that in both the word, the utterance, is not a mere symbol, but in itself a revelation, not merely a means but an end. The Word was God.

But, you say, we do have images brought before our mind in music. We have scenes suggested to us, and as we listen to a violin, or a piano, or an orchestra, we close our eyes, and we find rising up in our minds this vision or that which is appropriate to the spirit of the piece. We listen to the overture to Wagner's *Meistersinger*, and we are transported to the bosom of a deep forest, and hear all the spiritual utterance of wind and tree. Many listen to what is called the 'Moonlight Sonata' of Beethoven, and seem to see the moon rising over the waters, sailing up the sky, gliding from wave to wave of foamy cloud, and finally pouring from the zenith the splendour of her throned light. And so on infinitely, perhaps fantastically. The composers themselves, especially of late, have used effort to paint scenes with musical hues, and we have what is known as programme music. How can you say (I shall be asked) that music does not employ imagery? And, remembering the trains of congenial meditation which music has grown to stir in us, how can you say this art does not use the forms of thought? To which I try to answer. These images, these thoughts, are in music an effect of the artistic emotion, not, as in poetry, its cause. In poetry you grasp the images, the pictures, the situation presented by the poet, then you feel the delight. But in music the sound, the melody, the harmony rouse directly only the emotion, or the formless musical idea; which then takes shape in your mind in some image which you have once seen, and which has produced a like effect upon you.

No, music deals with pure and immediate emotion, vague, and delicious because vague. And perhaps we may go on to say that for this reason music demands less intellectual force in the artist than any other art. The great structural musicians are, I know, men of great intellectual power. But, for all the effects of music (and they are many) which do not spring from its structure as a vast artistic unity like the symphony, little intellect and more temperament is required, and the musician has to feel rather than to see or know. The painter, on the contrary, has to see as well; he must understand before he can interpret. Hence you find people sometimes of distinguished musical faculty, especially among *virtuosi*, who are quite ordinary, or less, in their intelligence, and quite devoid of intellectual interests. Music tends to be a self-absorbed art, and that sometimes to an extent which diminishes the musician's grasp of things, or his sympathy with others, and makes him the victim of great irritation, impatience, and intolerance. It is too subjective and ethereal to be as ethical as Art after all requires. This emotional and inward quality also predisposes the musician to a very lively religious devotion, but one frequently dissociated from intellectual and moral considerations. He therefore finds his religious home in Roman Catholicism, with its sacrifice of intellect, its transfer of responsibility, and its subordination of ethic to prescribed belief. We may further see in this quality of the musical art an explanation of the extraordinary precocity of musical talent. Mozart astonished his friends in his fifth year; Beethoven in his eighth; and Hummel in his ninth. The reason is that music needs little from without. No order of genius is so little dependent on personality and its moral maturity. It requires none of that familiarity with life and Nature which it costs painters and poets so much to acquire. It is simply the outpouring of an extraordinary endowment, where the personality may be little more than the pedestal of the genius, and the genius itself the instrument played by the Over-Soul.

Connected with the inwardness and spirituality of Religion is its *freedom*. The whole Infinite becomes the spirit's realm, home, and playground. So also in music. No other art gives such facilities for the free outpouring of the profuse strains of unpremeditated art. Every one will appreciate the force of this who knows the ease and delight of extemporising in music. The free fantasy flows forth untrammelled by the necessity of following a definite thought, or copying the features of outward things. The emotion is its own law, and supplies its own form. The painter has no such scope. His picture must be the reflection of something more than his own emotion. He reveals where the musician but inspires. His task is the harder one of conveying his feeling through the likeness of an outward thing or a group of things. Turner only tells all he felt to those who can read the secrets of landscape. He had to paint both himself and Nature, and to be true to both. But the musician, as he extemporises, has to express only himself. Sometimes the painter has envied the musician's freedom and vagueness so far as to make a daring effort in the same direction with his own art. He tries to paint, not things, but impressions. He produces what he calls Nocturnes—a term, observe, common to both painting and music. And Whistler has been almost as successful with his Nocturnes as Chopin with his.

Indeed, the spiritual and inward is so predominant in music, it is so subjective, so removed from outward or historic realities, that it comes to be more religious than either Christian or artistic. It is apt to pursue spiritual beauty, ignoring goodness on the one hand, and truth on the other. Christianity has, at its centre, an ethical genius, and an inseparable relation to historic and moral realities, which recalls the spirit from its flight of flame to the actual relations and sober junctures of life. It is, therefore, only in a limited way that Christianity uses music in its worship. And Art, in the greatest sense of the word, has a relation to Nature, and a firm, fine hold of the material element, which music tends to evade and escape. The term

Art, as you may have observed, is being rapidly confined to representative art, and to painting especially. And you will now see more reason for calling painting the most Christian of all the arts we have as yet considered, although it might be possible to say that music is the most religious. In modern art music expresses the Teutonic idealism, as painting does the Teutonic realism. The ideal element in national art leaves painting and passes into music. While the lively romance peoples add action and narrative to music, and make the opera. The opera is an effort on the part of music to supply its own defect of outwardness and individuality, and so to save its artistic life. Opera, as treated by Wagner, is the completest form of art, fusing music, poetry, and painting, and including in its *Weltanschauung* the tone, the word, the scene, the act, and an organic unity of thought.

I seem to find a connection between this vague and formless emotionalism, wherein lies the power of music, and the religious condition of our age, which, scientific though it is in all else, dreads to be scientific as to its religion, and dislikes whatever savours of distinctness and form, calling it dogma. No art is so popular to-day as music, and music never was so popular and so widely cultivated. For this, of course, there are many reasons. For one thing, music and poetry are the democratic arts in distinction from the aristocratic arts of sculpture, architecture, or painting, because these leave but single masterpieces which cannot be multiplied and can be monopolised, whereas song and verse can be indefinitely multiplied in performance and in print. But I think another reason may be this passion of the spiritual nature to-day to escape from intellectual and moral concentration of the kind which accepts objective control. It is not without significance here that music has become the religion of those who believe but in the kind of Supreme Being that lies behind the pessimistic systems of Schopenhauer or von Hartmann. That Being is the Unconscious, which made the greatest of all mistakes in stumbling into a defined and conscious world; and our grand aim must be to discard by an ethical process these limitations, and remerge into unconscious existence. And it is under the influence of music that a mind like Schopenhauer felt, *lege solutus*, a foretaste of that final and formless consummation. Few have written so deeply and finely as Schopenhauer of music as the religion of the godless soul, and as the earnest of the liberty of a lawless world. Positive science on the one hand and society on the other threaten to squeeze unchartered freedom out of life, and in desperation it retires to the citadel of music, and will not allow definition, limitation, or positive belief of any kind to approach the central seat of the soul. But that protest commits suicide when it goes on to deny to religion an intellectual side or a definite truth, and challenges the possible existence of any but an imaginative theology. Such people not only say that form shall not bind them, but they refuse its very needful power to steady them. It would be making the same mistake in Art to say that individual improvisation or temperamental fantasies were all that music could offer us, and that we should seek no more from her. Which is absurd enough in the face of those great musical structures which are bound into artistic unity by the stern control of intellectual power and constructive force. It would be like reducing all poetry to lyric poetry, lyric poetry to trills, and bards to birds. It would be excluding from poetry the epic or the drama, with their organic unity and intellectual grasp.

But probably, though this grasp and unity exists in the highest musical art, it is not that element which in music appeals to the great mass of even musical people. Few of them enjoy a long piece of music with any sense of its intellectual unity. Most of them love it because it transports them into a region where the actualities and limitations of real life have ceased to exist, and they are no more harassed by the demands of duty, the need of cohesion, and the obstacles of law. It becomes æsthetic self-indulgence. Now, for those who are in close, constant, and benumbing contact with worldly realities, this may be, from time to time, a great relief and blessing. But when it becomes the constant atmosphere of an otherwise idle life, or when its mere passive enjoyment absorbs the chief thoughts of people whose serious energy is called by duty elsewhere, then Bach gives way to Offenbach, and it may prove weakening to the best life in no mean degree. I speak of listening to music or dreaming at the keys. But if the individual become musically active, composing or performing, of course the danger is greatly decreased. If it is his duty to perform for others, or to compose on his own account, then he has active work of a more or less moral sort to do. And his position is that of a preacher who is to a great extent saved from the dangers of religious absorption by the need for study, on the one hand, and the duty, on the other, of reducing his thought and feeling to some outward and definite shape for the instruction and edification of his charge. The danger to the person of musical taste is that of living in a dreamy, will-less, and unreal world ; and as the bulk of musical people either play or hear for their own enjoyment the musical productions of others without becoming really active themselves, the moral dangers of the widespread musical taste are not insignificant. It is like sport pursued in the interest of the spectators rather than the athletes. High ethical authorities in Germany have looked with much distrust on the enormous musical enthusiasm of that people, as our own moralists view the spectacular sport that takes its place with us ; and they complain that it invites men, and especially women, to dwell to an enervating extent in a vague world of formless impulse, lawless emotion, vacant yearning, and impossible dreams. Perhaps, too, my remark about the affinity between the wide taste for music and the vague religiosity of the time may receive still greater confirmation from the religious condition of Germany than even from our own.

The dangers rising from music rise mostly from the popular use and treatment of it. But because these dangers exist they are not, therefore, radical to its nature. The excessive spirituality and remoteness of it from the world's interests and efforts, to be sure, is an inherent danger. But music is like religion in this, that it suffers more from its votaries than from its qualities. A great musician, however, like Bach or Beethoven is a man who gives to his art the seriousness of a noble or a colossal nature, and makes its pursuit a moral discipline of continual sacrifice and toil. There is an austere element of thought, law, and control in great music, which draws upon the gravest human energies and powers. There is a deep symphonic order in a truly great musical work which makes it of all things the best type of the infinite order and ineffable fulness of the cosmos. And there is a unity of melodic idea or theme flowing through it all which as fitly reflects the divine movement in the world, the thread of divine purpose, and the latent tendency or final destiny of human life. There is at once a compelling grasp and a pervasive idea in great music, which lift us, if we seek something more than mere amusement, into the vision which sees all things as working together for glory, good, and God. Music is a universal speech, not only in the sense of coming home to almost all hearts. In that sense it is true only of simple and homely music. But great music is universal in a deeper sense than the simple, as Christianity itself is. Its nature and destiny is universal. It sweeps over us with a wave of emotion which is humane, universal, and submersive of our own petty egotism. It exists to purify and organise the selfish emotions, not simply to soothe them, excite them, or indulge them. It lifts us into a world of things which includes our little aches and joys, laps them in a diviner air, and resolves them into the tides and pulses of an eternal life. It raises us to our place, if but for an hour, in the universal order of things, and makes our years seem but moments in the eternal process. It is not then our personal welfare we think of, or our private enjoyment. Music, like Scripture and Nature, is of no private interpretation. We feel then that our passions and affections, however real, are but rills and streams in an infinite world of love, sympathy, and consummation. All that limits us, hampers us, makes us less than catholic, is for the hour forgotten, and is as if it were not. Day by day in our ordinary life we rejoice in the acquirement of this good and that; we have had this pleasure, that success, the hope we set our mind upon, or the discovery we chanced to find. But there come seasons when we reflect thus: 'All these things have now lost their power to satisfy me, while yet they have left me with a deeper thirst than ever. The more I have of these good things, separate and private, the more I want of something not yet given. Single enjoyments do not fill me. If all my desires were met, would my soul be filled? Should *I* be satisfied? It is not enough that the things I gain should be my several private boons. They must bring with them some power to feed me on the heavenly scale, and raise my soul to its place in a general good and a final peace.' We look back on a long array of vivid pleasures and varied enjoyments, and we say to ourselves, ' So far good, but how far have they brought me on to the last goal, and made me the partner of an eternal gain?' We feel that there is a vast public, cosmic fulness of things, from which our private pleasures come like sparks or rays ; and, beyond all particular gifts, we long to possess this gift which holds of the Infinite and overflows the soul. We feel that there is one thing needful which we would choose with all our heart, that there is one pearl of great price which we would sell all our little jewels to possess.

In the region of science, for instance, it is one thing to know an ordered variety of facts or laws, another to realise the fulness and harmony of creation's life. The delight in a discovery is one thing, cosmic emotion is another. A savant might conceivably by disease lose some of his memory for facts, or his delight in laws. But he is happy if he has gained that greater sense, which nothing can destroy, of Nature's infinite fulness, grandeur, and resource. So is it in life. We seek to feel our private gains passing up into that infinite and common good from which they came, which in delighting each enriches all. We would live for a little there at least, and gradually gain the power of living more. Now this power Religion gives us in the supreme and permanent way. But music gives it us also in another way. Every sweet or mighty note melts into fine relation to a great whole, which presents us with a miniature, and bird's-eye view, as it were, of the world ; and we see it all working together in a spiritual symphony and forefelt harmony of conclusive bliss. Nay, it transports us for the time. And we enter as fleeting guests that house of the many mansions which another than an æsthetic power ensures us for the soul's dwelling-place for all generations.

So I say we have in a piece of great music the world's order in miniature. For if we survey this order, we discover three great elements entering into it. We find, first, the element of law ; then we find the element of matter and force in their various orders and forms, the things which obey the law, and so exist and work together in a harmonious way ; then we find, on a higher contemplation, the element of thought, the revelation or purpose, what Hegel calls ' the truth,' which is embedded in the totality of nature and life, which is evolving through it, and which it is the business of the poet, the philosopher, the prophet, and the saint, each in his way, to know and reveal. Now in music we have also three elements corresponding to these three. First we have the element of Time —like form in the plastic arts. That answers to Law. It is the steady, stern, commanding element, which acts like routine or duty in life, which must be observed, whatever be the seductive nature of the harmony or melody, and which in itself has little artistic power, but is the skeleton or mechanism that the art clothes with flesh. Secondly, we have the element of tone and harmony ; and that answers to the interaction of the various orders of things, forces, and souls, the clefs, so to say, which we find in Nature. The connection we have here is no more the ordered and stern connection of law, but the genial and congenial connection of affinity, or spiritual relation between tone and tone as between soul and soul. The world of Nature and of character is full of these affinities, and a great part of life consists in seeking and discovering them. Here lies the rich, deep power of music, one of the most Christian of its elements, because it corresponds most with the drawings of sympathy, brotherhood, and membership one of another. As an historical fact, musical harmony is a development of the Christian age and of the Christian Church, and partly because it offered musical expression for that sense of loving affinity and rich co-operation which is the Christian ideal for men, and the Christian revelation of Father and Son in God. Finally, we have the element of melody, or idea, or theme, which answers to the thought or purpose pervading, vivifying, and unifying existence, as a process not only organic and moving, but moving to one theme and one goal. The melody or idea, developed in countless ways through a long symphony or concerto, yet retaining its fugitive identity, is like a musical providence working itself out throughout the little world. Thus, as beyond all law, and beyond the affinities and harmonies of things, forces, and characters, deep in the structure of existence yet shaping it all, we have the vast divine idea or purpose of the universe, so also in music, distinct from the hard basis of time, and beyond the blending of rich harmonies, infused into all, and presiding over all, we have the melody or the musical idea, the theology of it—the same throughout, yet not the same, the more constant the more it changes, infinitely flexible, yet all comprehensive, ruling all while seeming to be poured out into the service of all for the sake of all. This is the greatest element in music as an art. It is in this that the power of the musical genius lies who is of the great prophetic strain. It is here that he exhibits at once his emotional and his intellectual power, his cosmic heart and understanding. But this is not the element in music by which it appeals to the great mass even of people musically sensitive. It demands too much concentration, too much exaltation, too much effort and spiritual habit. It seems too vast, severe, and distant for the sympathies of the bulk of men. If this were the function of music they prized, there would be little danger of its relaxing the moral fibre, sapping the power of thought, or creating a disgust with realities.

Such is my meaning in saying that music at its best presents us with the world in small. It gathers up our experiences and sets them in a universal order.

> Behold I dream a dream of good
> And mingle all the world with Thee.[1]

It gives us the inner sense of that cosmic catholic

---

[1] In Memorium, stanza CXXIX.

good, from which all that we have felt to be good has sprung. It is the art characteristic of our subjective, intimate, psychological age. It carries us through our subtle and vibrant selves beyond ourselves; and it makes us aware of vast relations, in which we take our rich part of ordered praise. And when we do profoundly realise this feeling, there is nothing but the speechlessness of music than can express it for us. 'Thought is not, in emotion it expires,' but in emotion which holds of the Eternal. When we have reached the region to which all nature runs up, the heaven which all our little pools of souls do but reflect in small, the pre-established harmony mirrored in each monad, then we do not seek to make pictures and similitudes of this or that in Nature or life. We call for some less fettered, some more prompt and spacious, utterance of our exalted soul than we find in the studious tracery of form or the reflective adjustment of colour. And we find word and wing in music.

This universal power of music makes it, in spite of the musician's tendency to self-absorption, the most sympathetic of all the arts; and were sympathy the whole of life it would be the art supreme. Nothing unites the two extremities of life, and calls the old man back to his child's years, like the echo of an early learnt and long-forgotten song, from the days before he crossed the world. No crowd of people before a picture feels the same wave of common emotion which sweeps over a musical audience. No oration can stir a whole nation like a song in which its own genius and aspirations get loud and fiery voice.

> When civic renovation
> Dawns on a kingdom, and for needful haste
> Best eloquence avails not; Inspiration
> Mounts with a tune that travels like a blast.

There is a vaster power in music, too, than in any other art of entering sympathetically into the shades and varieties of emotion; and this sets up a very close bond between the musician and his varied audience, and enables him, as it were, to pour his soul directly into theirs, duly dividing the word of power in flame that flickers on every head. And in worship it gives a facility for the common spiritual expression of unutterable things. There is no doubt the great bulk of church music ought to be such as the congregation can readily join. The art which best serves religious praise must be, like all the art which the religions delight most to use, simple and merely symbolic in its nature. I have once before referred to the devotion which gathered about rude Madonnas and crucifixes in comparison with the feeling stirred by Raphael's pictures. But it need not be exclusively so. As the congregation are ready to listen to a sermon from the preacher, they may likewise be prepared to listen to a brief sermon from a capable choir, when it is as reverent as it is musical. And the choir should feel that they occupy a middle place between preacher and congregation. If the words of their anthem or canticle are known to the congregation, that should be enough. It is not necessary that the congregation in this case should know or be able to join in the music. It may be better if they do not. The anthem is not part of the worship in the same sense as the hymns are. It should be regarded as a musical commentary or exposition on the words chosen; and as the congregation listens to the preacher speaking beautifully for thirty minutes on a text, so they need not grudge to listen for ten to the musical exposition of the same text by a devout choir. Nor need we object even to a solo in the anthem, except when there is the frequent danger that the artist thinks more of exhibiting his skill than of making sacred words more sacred and impressive. For this reason the vulgarity of naming the singer in the service should be suppressed. Here all self-exhibition is noisy impertinence. The same principles apply to the organ voluntary, especially the opening one. It is a chastened sermonette. It is an invitation to worship. Its object is to draw away our souls from worldly thoughts and modulate them into the spiritual key. If high music be not devotion, it is the next thing to it. It is the stepping-stone of the soul, if not to heaven, yet far above earth. The spirit has a shorter leap to enter the heaven of true prayer and holy thought than if we came straight from the sights of our streets, our gossipy thoughts, and the hurry of our indolence. First and last, the voluntary is part of the service; and there could be no better index, whether of taste or of devotional feeling, on the part of a congregation than that they should come in time for the one and stay for the other.

But, on the whole, it is not the very highest kind of music that is best fitted for use in Christian worship. Classical music, apart from its being above the comprehension of the great mass of worshippers, has not been found appropriate by the feeling and practice of the Church. And what is the reason ? Is it not this ? Classical (or shall we take the phrase ' absolute ') music is of the kind I described last when speaking of the three musical elements, the kind which develops the theme with rich variety, yet tenacious identity, through a long series of movements and phases. A symphony is the development of a musical idea. It is a kind of spiritual treatise on a musical theme, a piece of musical theology. The musical intellect works with power. And the effect of the whole is only felt by those who are able to appreciate the composer's persistent grasp. Now that is not the element which is made supreme in Christian faith, at least in worship. It is true the tendency of Protestantism has been that way; and we have its musical representative in Bach. But in worship at least, what is uppermost is another kind of unity—not of structure and thought, but of faith and love. It is not on the element of artistic symmetry, intellectual grasp, and organic completeness that Christian worship dwells. It is the element of sympathy, of unity which is not so much symmetry as harmony, uniting God and man in love, and joining in one chord different orders of character and energy; it is the affinity and concourse of spirits reconciled and made kindred, amid all their variety, by a common faith and love. The theme is a unity of thought; harmony is a unity of love. Therefore the worshipful element in music is the element of rich, deep, and varied harmony, not the severe control of a pervasive and developed melody. It is the old difference between Hebrew and Greek emerging again, forcing the choice which has made so much use in our worship of Hebrew hymns and forms—the form namely in which a sentiment or thought is not developed in an organic way, but repeated in a parallel way. A great lyric poem develops the poetic feeling from verse to verse; the Hebrew lyric—the psalm—repeats it in other words or images. Now it is the iterant psalm, and not the strophic ode, that gives the type for worship, and determines the ruling form of congregational music. Our hymn music repeats the same tune, with a fine iterancy, to each verse. Even when we pass beyond congregational singing, the form of musical composition which is specially ecclesiastical is not the symphony, which is Greek or Aryan in its organic unity of melodic growth, but the fugue, which is Hebrew in so far as that it does not develop the melodic phrase, or unfold the idea, so much as repeat it in varied harmony, as the psalmist repeats his idea in other images and words. The symphony develops, the fugue climbs. The fugue is a kind of musical sermon, in which the heart of the text is reiterated again and again in a new application, and not pursued into its logical significance and philosophic connections. It is 'half angel and half bird.' It renews the same deep sacred strain. It expresses the unity amid variety by a re-presentation of feeling, and not by an unfolding of thought. And as its object is more the aspects than the evolution of the theme, it has a freedom more like extemporising than the severe and studied form of classic compositions. It is not passionate, not charged with the immediate emotional effects at which more secular music aims. Its unity of love and harmony rather than of thought has an ethical rather than dogmatic quality; and it indicates the true nature of religious unity as one based upon spiritual concord rather than theologic accord. The repetitions of the fugue, its bursts of harmony answering to harmony and jubilance echoing delight, have been felt to be a fit image of the Gospel waking responsive praise from nation to nation over a whole redeemed earth, while heavenly hosts, in clouds of face and wing, take up the strain, and cast it from choir to choir in an infinite Hallelujah, because the Lord God omnipotent at length reigneth.

There is another feature by which music is allied to the offices of Religion, and that is the necessity for the constant reproduction of the musical work. Each performance has a relation to the composer's work parallel to that which many think exists between the Sacrament or the sermon and the work of Christ. So that reproduce is a misleading word.

It too easily is taken as if it meant repeat. The original and finished work is there once for all. It can never be repeated. Its finished and timeless universality can function afresh under the conditions of a given place or time. And little as it can be represented in its fulness, it can in some sense be re-presented. As it has no outward permanence, it must be recalled into evidence every time it is presented, by some living soul who is personally present. The composer must always have a living and personal representative. This is due to the directness and intimacy of the spiritual contact in music. As the material medium is fined away, so much greater grows the need for a close actual contact of spirit and spirit, presence and presence. The living soul must act directly on us. We cannot here be spoken to as the picture speaks. A living person is necessary to produce the musical effect—either the composer, or some other human being as his vicar, representative, and minister. And so it is in religion. The preacher or the priest intervenes. The spoken as well as the sung word of God produces its most powerful results when it comes through the living soul and sacramental lips of a fellowman. The preaching of the Bible has done as much for the Gospel as the reading of it. The press can no more supplant the pulpit (though it may confine it to the properly religious sphere) than the reading of music can supplant its re-production. Wherever the spiritual submerges the material to the extent it does in music and religion, the spiritual contact must again and again be renewed and made immediate by personal agency. And so we find that in those churches where the Sacrament of the word is submerged by the Sacrament of the bread, where a hierarchy, or a piece of palpable food is made peculiarly divine, and a material element thrust powerfully between spirit and spirit, the function of preaching retires into the background. The direct contact of spirit and spirit by the Word is impaired, or it is satisfied by preaching in music rather than in words. It is in those churches that a musical service has been carried to a great, and often to an unspiritual, perfection.

It would be possible to trace many more of the chief Christian and religious ideas in music than I have been able to set forth. But here there is some danger of becoming fantastic, and I will touch but on one or two points. And first I merely allude to what I have already named—the surrender and passage of the material to the spiritual, as the string vibrates into invisibility to make the tone. Second, I point out how music seems to fit the religion of the Cross, as we observe that in no art have unhappiness and eminence so often gone together. In no other art perhaps is the artist so straitened for his baptism, or so seeks his ideal sorrowing, to be rewarded only by the joy he finds in his art alone. And further, there is the idea of aspiration, the sense of infinite worlds not realised. No art, not even Gothic architecture, can so express the pathetic yearning of the soul for the

MUSIC

unseen beauty and the ideal good. No art so feels the inadequacy of the material to express or satisfy the longings of the spiritual. Indeed, this art impatiently, as it were, throws away the material altogether, and reaches out into heaven poised and resting by the merest tiptoe upon earth. In painting, the more rich and perfect the art, so much the more is the spirit detained upon it, and besought to tarry with the visible beauty, and not enter heaven yet a little while. But that is not so where the material is so evanescent as in music. We are passed forward almost at once into the spiritual world, and our aspiration is not delayed. That ceaseless aspiration, then, joined with abysmal rest, which is so peculiar a feature of Christianity, finds an expression in music more perfect than in any other outward means.

Further, there is a form of the idea of reconciliation which already we found to play so prominent a part both in Religion and Art. We have here, in music, matter and spirit, outward and inward, in almost complete fusion. In painting, the object and the spectator were held apart. Matter stood over against spirit. Before painting we contemplate something. But in music we are united with the work itself. It lives chiefly in the life of our spirit. We do not contemplate, we simply feel, feel what is poured into us, and absorbs us. The material base and the spiritual structure depend absolutely on each other, and are inseparable. And we have already seen how the emotional and the intellectual elements, which in our day are so sharply opposed, are in the highest music fused and reconciled. Love and law are in one accord. And many who have ceased to find peace in the reconciliation of Christ, find at least repose in the transfiguration of music.

But ' calm is not all, tho' calm is well.' And what the best music does not give is either certainty or finality. Too soon the mood, the vision, disappears, and from the glory of the mount we descend to the epileptics and disputes of this world. Art blesses the soul, but cannot save it. It cannot set us in the heart of a reconciliation assured for ever, or plant us in an everlasting redemption. Its power is evanescent, and can readily come to seem unreal. No wonder that music is not only the art of pessimism, but its religion. No wonder that pessimism, which at once seems to deepen the Christian note and to mock the Christian faith, has left as its greatest legacy the musical majesty and poignancy of Wagner. For the consolations of art are but fleeting after all, and pessimism sees but a spurious redemption in the process of things, and no reconciliation at all at their close—only a tragedy and pathos so great that it needs, even to feel them duly, the very God that the system rejects. To realise the tragic finale to which it brings the world, it ought to recall to the eternal throne the God of all power and love whom it discrowns and reduces to the greatest of all the redeemed—and erased.

True enough, there is a certain earnest of redemption in music, the uplifting and glorifying of human experience, the transfiguration of sorrow in a halo of musical beauty, and a brief straightening of crooked things, as an earnest and promise of the glory that is one day to submerge all woe. The great problem when uttered in great music is in some part answered. Like all art, music has preeminently the power to clothe the tragic facts of life in imaginative hues and robes of heaven. It redeems pain by showing it to us, existent indeed, yet absorbed, present, but lost in beauty and love, so that we can bear to look upon it, and even be soothed and strengthened by our gaze, instead of irritated and weakened, as we are by its bare and actual contact. Just as in Christ we see man with his sin and woe transfigured to goodness, standing through pain, and even through sin, on a height of glory not otherwise to be won, deified in a cross, and resurrection, and there determined as the Son of God with power, so in Art we see, for a time at least, man and his fate in spiritual and pacifying beauty. Art, in this respect, is the echo of Religion as the interpreter of life, nature, and destiny. Now this, which is more or less achieved by all art, is conspicuously accomplished by music. It soothes, transfigures, opens the fountains of a greater deep, and bathes us in a world of victory, which submerges our griefs so that we see them as lovely as ruined towers at the bottom of a clear lake on whose bosom we glide. It has, for the hour, the power that faith has for good and all—to unloose, emancipate, and redeem. When the ransomed of the Lord return to Zion, it is with singing and great joy upon their heads.

IX

POETRY

Much has already been said about the reconciliation in Art between Matter and Spirit. Because this idea of reconciliation, in some form, is as prominent in the philosophy of Religion as it is in that of Art. The object has been, not so much to trace the religious influences of Art, which is a matter giving rise to great variety of opinion; but I have rather striven to extract and exhibit, at times it may seem a little fancifully, the great ideas fundamental and common to both those great expressions of the soul. I have thought that, as these two spheres were the finest and most characteristic in the range of man's activity, we might by this analysis come upon principles lying at the root of Humanity, whose last secret is in its most subtle, rare, and hidden things. And I have thought, moreover, that it would be much gained if we could together see in each of those departments the redeemed unity and consistency of the human soul, both in itself and in its relation to God. I am open to be told by the plain man that I have been juggling with terms, or in some parts have seemed to do so, that I have been using this word spirit now with reference to the human soul, now with reference to God, and

POETRY

that I have skipped from the one use of the word to the other in a fashion which might seem to indicate confusion in my own mind, and produce the same in yours. But may I assure you there has been no desire to confuse, certainly none to juggle with terms, on my part? To go to the root of this matter would involve more theology or philosophy than would be in place here. I do believe that there is an essential unity between what is spirit in man and what is spirit in God, that the nature and constitution of man's spirit (I am not speaking of man's ruined moral will) reflects the constitution of the divine, and the movement of its process, and that the great ideas which rule in the human spirit are either the reflection or the complement of still vaster spiritual ideas reigning in the Divine Spirit. Spirit is one, our rational personal nature is one, however various be its conditions and manifestations, however rent may be our harmony of will. For my purpose in these lectures, therefore, dealing as they do with the relations between spirit and matter in the beauty of Art, I may perhaps use the term spirit as including either or both of its great modes, the human or the divine. Art, if it be an enthronement of the human spirit, is also a triumph and a revelation of the divine. The eternal value of Art is in proportion to its volume of spiritual idea and significance. I ought also to admit that the aspect of the soul which is turned towards Art is more pantheistic than that which turns to religion proper—to ethic, to faith, to action; and that if Art were our religion, nothing but pantheism would be left us for a faith—as is the case with all natures which are æsthetic rather than ethical in their tone.

What have we found, then, to be the part played by the various arts in respect of the soul? It is this. In architecture the temple contains the god. It is a wrap or garment, concealing more than it reveals, a mere shelter for the indwelling spirit, an inorganic body for it. The statue in sculpture sets the spirit forth and incarnates it. 'A body hast thou prepared me,' an organic, and, in one sense, perfect material form. The picture in painting does not so much incarnate the spirit as interpret an incarnation which has already taken place in creation in an inimitable way. Art can now but reflect and illuminate that as the Apostles did the finished Gospel; and in painting it points us on towards depths of spiritual life which it cannot fully incarnate and express, but which it can convey, and prove unspeakably to be. The song in music provides the soul with a spiritual vehicle; it gives, as it were, a fiery chariot to the sun; and, borne invisible upon invisible sound, spirit passes into spirit, heart melts into heart, the soul of man meets and embraces the soul of man in delight, and, speeding on the wings of the audible Word, the spirit of God enters and communes with the spirit of man. Music is, as it were, the ray of divine light which makes the soul vocal as it falls on it.

But what was the defect of music as art? It

was this, that it became too subjective; it got away too far from a real world. It became all inspiration, and no revelation. It gave up the idea of representing. Form became too rarefied. It did not work by representation, or sanctify form, but it acted by sound, with its direct transfer of emotion from soul to soul. And what was the defect of music as religion? This. That it tended to become too vague, dreamy, egoist, and unethical. It removed the soul too far from any memory or taste for the moral or other realities in life. It was also too fleeting in its joy and unstable in its effect. Moreover, the expressive power of music is limited. There are phases of experience which it does not voice readily, perhaps does not at all. For instance, like so many intensely spiritual powers or natures, it does not seem capable of expressing deep rich humour. It has plenty of comic resource of the *Figaro* sort, but is there anything in music like the deep humour which is most characteristic of Shakespeare, or any of the grand irony; which things have a real connection with the moral attitude to life? Painting, on the contrary, has these powers to a high degree.

With such defects, then, it can hardly be that music, deep and subtle as its power over feeling is, should head the procession of the arts. Art must recover what in music it lost, while at the same time it must retain what in music it gained. It must retain that subtle and pliant power of searching the caves of the soul, unlocking its powers, and drawing forth beauty like violets from its secret nooks and untrodden shades. But it must regain the power, lost in music, of keeping close to concrete reality, whether in Nature or in conscience, the power of realising to us our freedom through life, not through escape from it. To be free of reality is not to be rid of it. To be the world's freeman is not to rush out of the world. The freedom conveyed by music tends sometimes to resemble the freedom of a sack of incense which, being punctured by a fine instrument, is dissipated into fragrant air. The true freedom of Art, on the contrary, as of science, and of conscience, is not an escape merely, but the positive liberty of an exuberant power which bears lightly a load of thought or responsibility, and is braced by the cords which truss weaker flesh and cut into it.

To secure this end, Art must call in the element which in music it threw out. It must recall the representative or formal element. But it must, at the same time, follow out that growth in spirituality which we have seen to mark the procession of the arts. That means that the representation itself must be a mental or spiritual thing. It must be, and remain, a spiritual creation, not a material one. We must call back the pictorial art, but we must not paint on canvas, but on the mind, with neither colour nor sound, but with ideas. This was the task of poetry, in a way which I shall try to show.

Let me meanwhile, for a moment, make a little clearer what I have just said. You remember Greek art had two chief features. It was outward and material, not inward and spiritual (as we now understand spiritual). And it was typical, not individual; it dealt with types of beauty, not with shades of character, nor with expressive features. But when we come to Christian or Romantic art we find both those qualities of Greek art surmounted. We find art now to be inward and spiritual on the one hand, and, on the other, by consequence, it is quick and piercing to enter with a loving and faithful realism into shades of character, individual traits, and specific emotions, in dealing with each single object. Art expanded both towards the infinitely great and the infinitely small and fine. Now we saw that the inwardness and spirituality of Art went on growing as the material element fined itself away, till, in music, with the erasure of the material, we tended to lose the element of definite form, and get out of touch with the world and life. But what was this but to lose that other feature which distinguishes modern art, the feature of individuality, realism, and faithfulness. There was in music, to be sure, great growth in the subtle distinction of emotion in all its forms and stages. Yet against this subjective gain had to be set off the loss of like searching power with the outward half of existence. The purely spiritual, like a cloistered pietism, was overfed at the expense of its material consort. This element must be restored, but at the same time exalted in the process. The Art which crowns the edifice of Art must have the fine spirituality of music, but also the faithful drawing and colouring of painting, and both on another plane. This is the combination which is effected in poetry, with its rich imagery seen only by the mind's eye, and its searching ideas realisable only by imagination.

Now this advance [1] made by poetry upon both painting and music, in using the excellences of each to neutralise the faults of the other, seems to me parallel to a change which sometimes takes place in the religious sphere. It is said sometimes, with a vague grandeur which captivates half culture, that poetry is religion and religion is poetry ; and so we have all the realities of faith melted by the sleight and patter of some voluble conjurer into the final fabric of a vision, an airy, unsubstantial pageant of imagination. This is a loose and vicious use of words. Faith, indeed, is incomplete without imagination, and imagination is baseless without faith. But neither can stand for the other, or do its work. I may return to the distinction between them. What I try to point out here is that there is a modicum of truth in what these speakers say, though not exactly what they intend. What they intend is to dissolve the definiteness of Religion into the indefiniteness of poetry, and, by calling Religion poetry, they wish to redeem it from humdrum morality or tyrannous theology into the free change and lawless liberty of imaginative form. But for their purpose music would be a happier instance than poetry. For it is a salutary feature of religious feeling that it is abandoning the excessive formlessness which it had assumed in

[1] I do not refer to historic but to ideal sequence.

the hands of its most liberal and sentimental champions; and it is seeking to recover, if it has not actually found, an historic positivity which shall not be rigidly formal, a shapeliness which shall not be of iron mould, a system which shall be truly and morally rational, and a law which shall steady but shall not stunt its career. And this advance (as I think it) is parallel to the advance which is effected by poetry upon music. The tendency of music towards the abstractly spiritual, and to the erasure or neglect of individual and moral reality, I have already compared to a current tendency of religious thought. I compared it to that monistic tendency which, ever since Spinoza, and especially under scientific influences, has, during the whole of the great musical epoch, led thinkers to submerge the moral action of human personality in one grand process of homogeneous being, and so deny to man, as a personal unit, a permanent existence. This is a denial, or at least a begrudging, of that distinct and persistent individuality which is as essential to love as to art, and which poetry calls back at once to Art and to love in words like these:

> That each who seems a separate whole
> Should move his rounds, and, fusing all
> The skirts of self again, should fall,
> Remerging in the general Soul,
>
> Is faith as vague as all unsweet;
> Eternal form shall still divide
> Eternal form from all beside;
> And I shall know him when we meet.

> And we shall sit at endless feast,
>   Enjoying each the other's good.
>   What vaster dream can hit the mood
> Of love on earth?[1]

To say, then, that religion is poetry would really be, if we measured our words, to re-import into religion with salutary vigour that element of definite and eternal form which seemed in danger of passing into a general being as featureless as the sky, and a catholic emotion as facile as the wind. Undogmatic Christianity is mere music; it is not even poetry.

I may also remark in passing that we see in practical affairs this same tendency which I have described as dangerous to both Religion and Art. In politics it would be hard to say which system crushed or ignored the individual more, the Imperialism of Bismarck or the Socialism of Lasalle; the despotism of the Czar, or the Nihilism which blows it up; the Militarism of the French Second Empire, or the Communism which it engendered, and which tried to repeat, when its time came, the lesson it had been taught by its tyrants.

A few words as to the really sensuous element in poetry, in order to make clear its place in the process of rarefaction which I have tried to show going on in the development of the arts. In music we at length left the outward hanging to the inward by a single sense, so to speak—the sense of hearing. It is the same sense that we depend on to a large measure in poetry. Both arts employ sound. But mark what a different place the

---

[1] In Memorium, stanza XLVII.

sound occupies in the one and in the other. In music it is a tone, in poetry it is a word. We must have some sensuous element in all Art, else it ceases to be art; but the object in artistic development is to transcend, rarefy, and throw down that element as much as possible, consistently with exalting in a real way the ideal and spiritual element. The competition among the arts, so to speak, is like a tea race between China clippers. It is to combine the maximum of spiritual cargo with the minimum of material tonnage. Now, in this respect the other arts are left behind, and the struggle lies between music and poetry. Both vessels, to carry on the metaphor, are built of sound. But in music the sound is an end in itself. It is elaborated, embellished, raised to the highest pitch of artistic beauty. It is as if the ship were made of mahogany or walnut, with every plank polished till it shone, every surface carved, and all the metal burnished till it gleamed. The lines of the craft are as much or more of an object than its carrying qualities. In poetry, on the contrary, though everything in the vessel (in the element of sound, that is) is ship-shape and sailorlike, it is the carrying quality that is most in regard, the power of conveying ideas and images in the most vivid way. The sound (as word) is merely a means. The sensuous element, instead of being erected into a delightful end, is reduced to a means and thrown down as a base. Or if it is raised into a structure, it is merely a scaffolding, it is not the building itself. To take an example; in Shakespeare's *Othello* it is the character of the Moor, or of Desdemona, that is the poet's real artistic creation, not the words of the actor, artistic though they are, by which he conveys the character to us. But in opera, in Verdi's *Otello*, the sound, the music, is much more vital to our impression of the people and the events involved. It is not solely the spiritual forms of the characters that live within us and raise our emotion to such a pitch; it is also the sensuous sounds by which they are recited to us. So the poetry of the *Divine Comedy* lies only in a secondary way in the art of the style. Indeed, we may see for how little comparatively this latter element may stand in poetry if we reflect that a poem may be either read or heard, taken in by eye or ear, that it may without entire loss be translated from one language to another, and that it may appear in verse or in prose, and yet not be wholly ruined as a poem. Some think, indeed, that good prose translations of foreign poems are after all better than verse.

It is therefore, perhaps, not extreme to call poetry the most perfect of all the single arts. It includes in some fashion all the rest. It reconciles them, and in reconciling them it raises them to a higher sphere. It is musical, picturesque, statuesque, architectural. For it is melodious, and it is representative either of complex pictures or of single forms, and it is structural, it is built into great intellectual and æsthetic wholes. It is superior to painting in inwardness, to music in outwardness. It is representative, and it is nonrepresentative, and it is both on the higher plane of the mind alone. It is representative, but it is also inward; and by combining these two qualities it is able to go deeper than painting, and to represent what painting cannot do. It can, by virtue of its inward, subtle, and sympathetic quality, give us the representation of a growing action or a developing character. It can penetrate the texture of the heart, and express in more intimate psychology than any art the delicate shades of individual character and the successive stages of spiritual process. To the definiteness of painting it adds the mobility and liquidity of music, and it thus enables us to follow the windings of a heart as it either expands or shrinks, or the tides of an action as it waxes or wanes. Painting can but seize and immortalise a moment; music can but embody emotion; poetry, on the other hand, can seize a whole soul and character, with its moral complex of emotion, intellect, and will; and it can show us this soul, not in one stage or at one moment, but developing through many stages, and rising or falling through days or years. Of all poetry the most perfect is dramatic poetry, and it is this which the drama enables us to do. It gives us, not only the anatomy and physiology of a character, so to say, but its biology. It not only analyses and presents, it creates. It tracks and exhibits the growing life, and, alone of all art, it can, like God, create a fellow being, who henceforward lives with us and sometimes rules us, elicits our love, our admiration, or our pity, and even has power, in no mean degree, to shape our characters and our lives. More than any other art does poetry thus approach the universal range of religion. There is nothing in human life that it may not handle. Its imagination ranges from heaven to earth, from earth to heaven. And all the contents of earth and heaven it bathes in preternatural light. We and ours are then transfigured, as if the potsherds of earth and its oozy stones were seen at the bottom of a clear and limpid well. If truth lies at the bottom of a well, poetry is the water that covers and transfigures it, while it refreshes and restores. This, of course, is the function of all art, but none is able to cover so much with its flowing medium as poetry. Architecture, sculpture, painting, music, all had a limited circle, to which their material confined them, but poetry casts its spell on all men and things, on the whole man and the sum of things. It is charged with the mission of universal redemption in the artistic sense. It loves whatever interests the human soul. And thus it comes nearer than any art to that spirit of infinite and redeeming love which is the soul of religion.

And this, too, might be noted. The higher that art rises in the scale of refinement the more comprehensive it is, as is the case also with religions; and they are the true foes of both who would make them the appanage of a clique or of a sect, the peculium of a school or a theology, the preserve of specialists, or the property of a set. Like Scripture, it is not the possession of a single nation.

Like the truest religion, also, it has a vast variety of national forms, and it embodies the aspiration and the visions of the most diverse and distant ages. It was religion as Christianity which, in waking modern European nationality, awoke also a national poetry and literature. And as some have spoken of a Christianity as old as Creation, so the very catholicity of poetry has made it, though the crown of the arts, not the last to arise, but a growth of every age, existing alongside of the other arts, and as if it were their spirit and providence, besetting them before and behind. The existence of Homer at one end and of Shakespeare or Goethe at the other end of the poetic line causes serious difficulties to any one who would trace the growth of poetry as they might that of the other arts. But all the spiritual products offer a like difficulty to those who would rigidly apply the formula of evolution. So here again we have an analogy and an affinity with Religion; and we have a reply, if not an answer, to those who cannot admit the claim of Christ's revelation to be unique, and, in its sphere, final, because, being fixed in the historic past, He must be but a stage and factor in a universal development which will one day leave Him behind. Does history not warrant us in saying that the converse may be more true? Are there not regions of spiritual activity, and incarnations of spiritual energy, which make us feel rather that any law of development as yet formulated is itself not final? And, indeed, till we have a purview of the whole field of time for our induction, future as well as past, can we ever call any law of development final, as against the revelation of God, the inspired witness of genius, and the intuitions of faith ? But one thing. Whatever difficulties the history of poetry or of religion may place in the way of the development theory as final and universal, there are features in both which suggest an affinity between them and that theory. As the revelation of the Infinite in Christianity gives us a boundless field and an exhaustless force for development, so the subtle flexibility of poetry, and its power to represent developing action or character, make it, in a special way, the art which science might use when she would put on her beautiful garments and break forth into believing joy. Science especially, with its modern methods and results, may be the contrast, but is not the contrary of poetry. Opposite they may be, but they are not contradictory. If the history of man be a drama, the history of the Universe might be set forth as an ' Ode of Life,' by some future and Christian Lucretius.

Of all the arts, then, perhaps we may say that poetry is the most truly religious. And this is not only shown by the philosophy of each, it is also indicated by the part which poetry plays both in our religious sources and in our religious services. Whatever controversy may be stirred about the place of carving, painting, or music in worship, one thing is beyond controversy, that the Bible, and especially the Old Testament, is largely poetical,

POETRY 241

and that it proceeded from a people whose habits of mind and forms of speech were poetic to the exclusion of every other imaginative form. This seems a very harmless and patent statement. But the harm that has been done to Religion by its neglect is great. The literal and scientific mind of the West has thrust its dogmatic categories upon the fine blossoms of Oriental piety, and they have been withered by the touch. They have lost the fragrance, both of Religion and of Poetry, crushed by this ungenial hand. The Rose of Sharon lay trampled and soiled beneath the feet of these intellectual crusaders of the West. For ages this desecration of the garden of the Lord went on, and the Eden of the heart was lost because men would eat in it of the Tree of Knowledge rather than of the Tree of Life. It was only at the end of the eighteenth century that men really awoke to the treasures and beauties of Hebrew poetry; and the great Herder may be said in this respect to have rediscovered the Bible, as the critics have done since from another side. When the fragment of a poem charged with Eastern hyperbole was taken as an actual narrative of the sun and the moon standing still; when the expression 'Let us make man,' in the beginning of Genesis, was used as a proof of the doctrine of the Trinity; when the Eternal Sonship of Christ is found proved in a lyric poem called a psalm, which is really an ode to a Jewish king; when the whole philosophy of the Atonement is discovered fully developed and embedded in a passionate prophecy like a fly in amber; when the imaginative visions of Daniel, or Ezekiel, are taken as a programme of the future, as history delivered in advance, and annals by anticipation of the world's close; when the mystic visions of the Apocalypse are treated as conundrums or ciphers, and reduced to figures on a slate, and the procession of subsequent history unfolded by the application to this book of some system like those which flourish at Monte Carlo—when such things are done with books and with a people imaginative and poetic, what must be the reflex action upon the mind that does them? Must it not mean some, and often much, blunting of sense for their true treasures, and the ruin of their divinest meaning and worth? If we will drag scientific laws from a lyric poem, and future history in its particulars from a passionate wail, what can we expect to leave behind us but débris? And that is just the conception that numberless people have of those parts of the Bible which a true sense deems among the finest. They read it on the flat. There is no beauty in it that they should desire it. No, because they have found only the grey débris, the broken crucibles, the dead ashes, the crushed fibre that the scholastic chemist left behind when he had done extracting and bottling the elixir of those flowers of imagination and faith. Whatever they may have done for the New Testament, many theologies have well-nigh ruined the Old. And the theologians of the future have their work to undo in this regard.

It is not as if in the inspiration of these poetic books there is now no revelation. On the contrary,

POETRY 243

there is there a greater revelation than ever for us, but we have much mistaken it. Inspiration and Revelation are two very different things, and one mistake we have made has been to treat them as being co-extensive, if not identical. The first mistake, of course, was in applying such words to a book. It is said the Bible is a revelation from God, or the Bible is inspired. The statement is loose. The Bible *contains* God's revelation (though in no dissectible way); what *is* the revelation is the Gospel, as some put it, or, as others would say, Christ, or the line of historic redemption. And, as to Inspiration, it is not, strictly speaking, the Bible that was inspired, but the souls of the men whose writings fill it. The more we dwell on this, the more we may feel what important consequences flow from the correction. The verbal, literal infallibility of Scripture goes down at once, for example, and with it so many of the doubts, or attacks, it has roused. But we are now well forward with more just and reasonable views on this matter.

The second mistake is less easily set right. It has been, as I said, to make Revelation and Inspiration cover the same ground, and to suppose that everything a Bible writer said under his inspiration was to be taken as a revelation, and placed beyond question. The difference between the two is that inspiration is subjective; it is a state—an exalted state of the spiritual and imaginative faculties; whereas revelation is objective; it is the burden or base of truth and superhuman reality which the inspiration holds, as it were, in solution. The same molten state of inspiration holds suspended in it both gold and dross, both passing error and permanent eternal truth; and a great amount of inspiration will yield sometimes only a percentage of real and eternal revelation. To take the Bible as a whole, it is the record of a vast and voluminous inspiration, which fused up in its heat a whole mass of human interests, passions, beliefs, ambitions, and errors; but it is not impossible, as every Christian knows, to extract from the mass the pure gold of the historic, superhistoric, and eternal revelation of the holy love and free grace of God in Christ Jesus our Lord.

The difference between Inspiration and Revelation is like the difference between music and poetry, between the sound and the word. Music, with its state of exaltation, its lack of definite or abiding form, and its inability to convey purpose or certainty, is inspiration by sound; poetry, with its representations, its thought, its imagination, or mental definiteness of form, and its power to convey a moral teleology, is revelation by word. The one places us in an exalted, emotional, and inward state. The other not only does that, but conveys to us the intelligible interpretation of real and outward acts. Not their reality, observe, but their interpretation. The parallel only goes so far. Poetry, though revelationary, is not chiefly concerned with revelation. That is, its prime object is not to assure us of the absolute reality of those forms of thought, purpose, feeling, or character which it marshals before us. It is to

POETRY

impress us with their power or beauty. Their reality is prime for revelation (whose object is certainty), but it is subordinate for poetry. It is an element that must be there. If they were obtrusively unreal, the poetic effect would be lost. The reality, however, is not the element uppermost in our consciousness under poetic enjoyment or activity. When that element of reality does become uppermost, while the beauty is made secondary, we are in the domain of Religion. Pure fiction, provided it is only real in substance and idea, can be poetic, but pure fiction, however probable, cannot be in the strict sense religious. It cannot give us certainty. It is religion which gives us absolute assurance of the reality in some form of those good or beautiful visions called up by poetry. It is faith, as faith in fact, which guarantees the reality of those poetic imaginations which we so love that we long to find them true. It is faith which fills the forms and images of poetry with substantial truth, and anchors them by us on the rock of reality, of God. It is religion more than poetry which teaches us to say:

All we have hoped, or dreamed, or willed, of good shall exist;
Not its semblance but itself; no beauty, nor good, nor power
Whose voice has gone forth, but each survives for the melodist,
When Eternity affirms the conception of an hour.
The high that proved too high, the heroic for earth too hard,
The passion that left the ground to lose itself in the sky,
Are music sent up to God by the lover and the bard;
Enough that he heard it once, we shall hear it by and by.[1]

So you see how fit and happy (however partial) is

[1] Browning: Abt Vogler.

that New Testament definition of faith as the substance of hope, the realisation of the unseen, as grasping the element of reality in imagination, of revelation in inspiration.

And finally, when the element of reality is not only uppermost but alone, when the element of emotion or beauty or trust is absent, we have philosophy, we have metaphysic. Religion then, we may see, blends all the faculties in supreme accord. It is musical in that the element of pure emotion takes a prominent place. It is poetical in that it has an imaginative vision of beauteous forms and images of good beyond our emotion. It is philosophical in that it is real and has the passion for reality. But it is what it is, it is religion, in that it blends all those in an attitude of will, while keeping uppermost the sense of reality and the assurance of faith, in the practical form of personal certainty and trust of a Person.

Now the task in dealing with the Bible, and especially with the Old Testament and its poetic parts, is to distinguish the Inspiration from the Revelation, the human from that which is divine as well, the prophet's racial tradition from his spiritual creation, what starts with man and reflects him from what starts with God and reflects Him, the imagination from the faith. In the prophets this is especially necessary. They clothed their certainty of faith, their absolute belief in God and His fellowship, in a moral order and in a final kingdom of righteousness—they clothed that faith, I say, in brilliant dreams of the national imagination,

POETRY

and hues of their own fresh borrowed from the heart. They had a small horizon compared with ours, but (and partly for that reason) the volume and force of their insight was vaster than ours; and they are mediums by which, when we have allowed for their imagination, we are made receivers of a real revelation and partakers of an eternal faith. How truly this separation of imagination from faith in the Bible is the task of our day may be seen in the great controversy about the personality of God. Take a poetical critic like Matthew Arnold. His whole contention in his influential books about the Bible was that the Jewish view of God as a person is a projection of the national imagination on the screen of the invisible. The Divine Personality was removed by him from the region of faith or revelation to that of imagination, and held to be one of those human errors floating as dross in the molten inspiration. The belief in a moral order, on the contrary, he would say, has real outward validity. It is not a mere imagination. It may be clothed in imaginative shape, but it is itself to be retained within the sphere of faith. It is a real revelation to us, verifiable, sure, steadfast, insuperable by the growth of knowledge or the lapse of years. When our earthly house and tabernacle of imagination is dissolved, that righteousness, he would say, remains a house not made with hands eternal as the heavens.

The difficulty of the present day, then, in respect of our religious and poetic documents, is not so much to get rational people to admit a distinction in Scripture between substance and form, Faith and Imagination, Religion and Poetry; but it is to get them to agree where to draw the line. There is a line to be drawn; that is a great step in advance. The work of the hour is to fix the delimitation by an informal commission of those qualified by study, taste, and faith to deal with so delicate a point.

There is one feature which I have named as common to both religion and poetry, and which renders their distinction a delicate matter. I mean the fact that both manifest themselves in an inward and spiritual picture, or mental image. The conspicuous feature of poetry we found to be the inwardness of its conceptions. Its visions and descriptions are seen only with the inward eye. But of this kind also are those ideas of Religion which are something more than poetry, and which are of the nature of revelation. How are we to distinguish between our ideas, and part those that are simply our own from those that have an objective worth, and are really inspired by God? Into this question as regards our private lives I do not here enter, but it reappears in connection with the interpretation of Scripture. The erroneous notions, the poetic imagery, and the real abiding divine revelation are all alike inward, and of the soul alone. It was no audible voice, it was no printed page, that came to Abraham as the voice of the Lord. It was an inward inspiration; and he very nearly committed an awful crime by his inability at first to distinguish the false in his impulse from the true. It was an inward and poetic vision that passed before the spirit of Isaiah as he saw the city of the Lord exalted on Zion, and the nations flocking thither with their homage. But only part of that vision was true. The precise form of its imagery, which I do not doubt the prophet himself believed would be realised, never has been and never will be actual.

The vision of Paul, again, at Damascus to many minds was not an outward and ocular vision at all. No man could see it but himself. It was subjective. It was to his own eye that the form of the Crucified appeared. It was in his ear alone, as in Abraham's case, that the strange words rang. But I have just as little doubt that the vision was real, that it was not a mere projection, and not a mere hallucination rising from a morbid, nervous condition or a sunstroke. If these things played any part they were but concomitants. I think the revelation was real, and that Christ did speak to Paul, with all, and more than all, the reality and force He would have had if He had stood forth in the sight of the Apostle's companions, and made His words audible to them as well. This was a case, not of imagination, but of revelation. It was something more than a mere projection from the Apostle's interior. It was inward, but it was objective none the less. And it was not imaginative, it was spiritual reality of the kind that changes life and history.

I might have divided the discussion into three parts, and I might have spoken about (1) The religion in all poetry, (2) Religious poetry, (3) Ecclesiastical poetry, or psalms, or hymns. The history of these and the examination of their relations would be both interesting and fertile. But in a single lecture it is best to deal as far as possible with the essence of the subject. If it is asked where the Christianity of poetry is to be sought for, the answer might be this. It does not lie in its direct Christian ends, but in the spirit which pervades it in pursuing its own proper ends, and also in the structure of the art as shown in the ideas pervading it. I have to your weariness pointed out the play of some of the great Christian ideas in the structure of the fabric of art. With these ideas *as doctrines*, Art, and especially poetry, has nothing to do. She does not make a direct study of them, or seek to enforce them. She is built upon their foundation, they are in her tissue, but she does not wear them on her forehead. It is the ruin of Art to become theological or doctrinal, as we saw in Byzantine art, and as we see in the poetic poverty of many hymns. Art has great Christian ideas, as theology has ; but Art has them in a latent and unconscious, though formative way ; whereas theology, or scientific religion, brings them to the surface and is intensely concerned with their handling ; while experimental religion appropriates them as the content of the soul's life. They pervade Art like the laws of life, of which a healthy body is unconscious, though thereby it exists happy and free. Poetry, like all true art, must have no direct end outside itself, *i.e.*, outside the aim of realising to us the beautiful by inward images, and exciting the appropriate emotions. It impresses, it does not convert or proselytise. If it had another aim, then there would be two supreme ends before it, and out of their collision would rise a discord fatal to Art; or if both ends were not supreme, Art would become a means only, and not an end in itself. It would become a means of edifying us in a religious way. And that for Art would be a degradation, as we see in the case of a multitude of religious pictures and tunes. If the religious effect is uppermost, Art is degraded, and Religion, in the end, is not served. Poetry, therefore, must not aim at a distinctly and directly religious effect. It has a religious element, and it has a religious effect. But these are incidental. In the so-called religious poems which are also great in point of art, it is not the religion, far less the theology (say, of the *Divine Comedy* or *Paradise Lost*) which have given them rank and immortality in literature. It is the imaginative, and not the edifying treatment of the great issue of life. They impress on us in a beautiful way the great spectacle of things; they do not force on us our personal relations with it. The very theology is presented as an imaginative fabric, and not in a dogmatic interest. And such poems do us a great service, not by presenting matter for our faith, but by enabling us to appreciate the æsthetic grandeur of those speculative systems by the loss of which religion is often so trivial and poor. In the world of art we are in a region distinct from the religious, kindred though they are; and influences pass from the one to the other if each have free scope to be itself. They co-operate best like citizens in a free state, by the free individual development of each. They are united in no outward hierarchy, but by a common spirit. They are distinct realms, so to speak, in the concert of civilisation.

And it is not religious ends only whose direct pursuit is forbidden to poetry, but every other end except its own. Poetry has a powerful moral influence, but it is injured as poetry when it becomes a lesson or a sermon. There are political and national principles in poetry, but if poetry aim straight at a political end, it must not aspire to rank as Art. And so there is amusement, relaxation, in poetry, but it kills the art if it be made to minister to these ends in chief. All those objects poetry can help, and help perhaps more than the other arts, but only indirectly. It must be true to its own vocation, its own genius. It must finish the work given it to do. Just so a woman may not unsex herself for any righteous cause; and a man who serves his country must be true to himself, and must seek no end for that country's good which would do fundamental violence to his own nature or conscience, or cause him the loss of his own self-respect.

And, therefore, we need not deplore the fact that poetry is so humanistic or naturalistic. That itself is, to a large extent, a result of the humane and genial side of Christianity, the side which gave the new religion so much affinity with Greek culture and thought. But further than that, the humanism of the Christian age is a very different thing from the humanism of Greece. It has depth, tenderness, heart, and soul as Greece had not. And it is now found impossible, in spite of splendid efforts by geniuses enamoured of the antique, to make classic poetry, or its more successful imitations, satisfy the romantic longings of the modern heart. Milton's *Samson* is more classic than Goethe's *Iphigenia*, or Swinburne's *Atalanta*. The Infinite Love has dawned on men, and those hear its music who cannot decipher its character or understand its words. There is another echo in our ears as we close a Shakespearian play from that which besets us as we lay Sophocles down. It is no less sad, perhaps, but it is far more deep, more rich, more wide and varied in its chords. Modern tragedy has a different reverberation in spiritual space. The life which in both may be crowned with gloom is in key different for each. And there is a subdued hope and a chastened promise in the pathos of the modern drama which is absent from the unrelieved pity and blank fate which ended rather than rounded life for the ancient heart. The life, which to Shakespeare is rounded with a sleep, is to Attic tragedy crushed by Fate or snapped by hopeless death. Between Sophocles and Shakespeare there is the whole spiritual world of Christianity. And we may, perhaps, say that if the Greek poet was, in an artistic and unconscious sense, the prophet of Christ, the English is one of His apostles. Finally, after all I have said, this modest maxim at least will probably not be challenged: 'All true poetry has something Christian in it, and all true Christianity has something poetic.'

X

ART, ETHIC, AND RELIGION—I

THE religious, or the moral, element in Art lies less in what you paint than in how you paint, less in the subject than in the handling, and in the ideal handling rather than in the devout. The religious artist is not to be confined to religious subjects, nor even to distinctly religious ideas. Nor have we religious art simply because it comes from a devout man who never sat down to his easel without a prayer. It is certain that much verse which never touches art or inspiration issues from the devoutest men. Nobody, of course, pretends that devotion is a guarantee of artistic technique. But just as little does it ensure artistic vision. To love Christ is not to love Nature. To see into Christ is not to see into beauty. St. Paul had no sense of natural beauty whatever. Faith does kindle imagination, and does give a man insight. Think of the imaginative insight in the idea of the Church and Christ which makes Ephesians a spiritual symphony, a great theologic ode. But faith does not give a man the kind of insight that is the artist's gift and power. We care less for the spirit in which a man paints or composes than for what he sees and has to convey. What he gives us is not directly what he is, but what he receives.

If I were to use the language of theology, I should say the stress lay not in his inspiration, but in his revelation. Feel he must, but it is not how much he feels, it is what he feels. It is not the quantity of his excitement, but its quality, its content. Inspiration is a subjective thing. It has to do with the physical condition of the artist. But the great object of great art is not to give us the artist's temperament, nor let us know how it could flame. It is to use that temperament to convey something. The artist gives us not himself, but his own order of truth. If the artist's aim is to exploit Nature in order to exhibit himself and display his inspiration or his skill, it ruins Art. It kills Inspiration. It is in Art as it is in Religion. The adventurer is the man who exploits Art or the Church for his own career or genius; the apostle is one who serves Art or Church for its gospel. It is only the very lowest forms of Art, like the acrobat's, that depend on self-exhibition. The true artist has this much from the Holy Spirit—' He shall not speak of himself.' Art is not there for the artist. It is not there to reveal his temperament. It is to let us see Nature through a temperament—which is a very different thing. It is not good for Art when the public makes more of the actor than the part, and of the artist than of his work. His message is the great thing. What matters is not the seer, but the thing seen. Great art is revelation. It is objective. Whereas inspiration is sub-

ART, ETHIC, AND RELIGION 257

jective. Now, in religion or ethics, the main interest is not the subjective but the objective. It is not how we believe or obey, but *what*. That determines the how. It is not how we feel that is of first moment, but what we feel, what makes the feeling, and whether we feel worthily what we see and say. It is not the experience, but the power which creates it that means most for us. Is the sentiment honestly produced by the object? Does it honestly correspond to the reality? Is the feeling worthy of the worship? That is the moral and the religious question. And if Art also is to be really great, if it is to be religious or moral in its own way, it must be so by its objective content, its word, its revelation, by the thing seen, and not by the gleam in the seeing eye. So that from this point of view I just reverse what I began by saying. The religion of Art lies not in how we paint, but what we paint, meaning, however, not now the subject, but the message, the interpretation of it, conveyed. It lies in the artist's manner of conceiving and construing a world.

All art is sacramental in its nature. Does not the artistic temperament notably gravitate to the most sacramentarian of the churches? The artist has a certain vision, which he embodies in a certain material form, with the object of conveying to poor me the same vision or the same mood. The outward is used by his inward to rouse a like inwardness in me. But his sacramental use of the outward is more than memorial, more than symbolic. He incarnates his vision, he does not merely suggest it. There is a certain transubstantiation. He does not simply *associate* his feeling with the material, nor symbolise it, but he embodies his feeling in the material. His material assumes a form prescribed, nay, compelled, by the nature of his idea. In Art the work clothes the idea like a skin it produces, and not like a garment it throws on. Hence, in Art also (as in the central rite of the great æsthetic Church of Rome), the sacramental element acquires a permanent and eternal value for itself. Here the symbolism of Art differs from that of a more ethical religion. There the material symbol is associated with the idea rather than organically changed or created by it. It is its adjunct, and not its body. It suggests it, but does not express it. And the grace is conveyed, not by the elements, but by the act of faith which handles them in a communion of Christ's act. But in both cases the material is there for a purpose beyond itself. In Art it brings together in a high and joyful way the artist's genius and my soul, and enables me in some measure to hear what he hears and see what he sees. It reconciles me for the time to my world. It makes me the citizen of a world unseen. The material is there, not for the satisfaction of sense, however refined, nor for the rousing of memory, but to bring about some communion of spirit between me on the one hand and the artist's interpretative genius on the other—nay, rather, with the world, the idea, or message with which he is charged.

So far there is much in common between Art

ART, ETHIC, AND RELIGION

and Religion, or conscience. But there is a difference. The one will not do the work of the other for the soul. Art ministers to insight and its joy, religion to conscience and its faith. Religion lies nearer than Art to the conscience, or to the Cause, of what ought to be and shall be.

II

We say the artist has to seize the *idea* of what he represents and convey it. And he is also inspired continually by the *idea of perfection*. But what does that mean?

Immanent, but mostly buried in material nature, there is a spiritual something beyond the ken of the senses alone; and Genius raises it from the grave and reclothes it with a new and finer body, which gives it access to us in a way that Nature failed to do. At the great word Lazarus comes forth. What the artist sees entombed within material nature he raises and reveals to us by a Nature above Nature—by his genius. The artist gives to the spiritual a more perfect translation than Nature did, because to Nature he adds that supreme energy of Nature which is human genius. The spiritual something beyond Nature or Genius, and using both, we might call its Idea (if we are careful to think of an idea as a reality and a power, and not as a dream). And the artist is always toiling to perfect by his technique Nature's expression of that idea as well as his own, and to complete Nature by soul, as God completed it in man. He does more than represent Nature, he interprets it, and he does not imitate it at all. But he does more than even interpret; he completes Nature. ' For Nature is made better by no mean, but Nature makes that mean.' He certainly does not impose himself on Nature. It is a pathetic fallacy to say that ' we receive but what we give, and in our life alone does Nature live.' It is not the artist's own idea imported into Nature. That would be mere fancy. It is Nature's idea uttered, and completed, and coming to itself through the artist. That is real imagination. And such is ideal art. ' If an artist paint a lion with genius, his success is not in the mere copying of the creature; but that creating nature which brought the lion forth meets the creature again with the imagination of the artist, and continues in the picture the same work that began the beast.'

But we speak continually, not only of the ideas in the world, but its ideals. We may give to the idea of the world a meaning beyond its urgent cause or its rational structure. We may see in it the final stage and consummation. We may mean not only a Sabbatic idea that reposes within Nature (or man), or feels its way out through it, but the final idea to which the whole creation moves, the great divine event Nature is working out, what closes and crowns Nature and History, the Idea in its final consummation. We may mean not only the idea in the world, but the ideal it moves to, its final destiny rather than its inner self.

But are these two, the idea and the ideal, not at bottom the same? Ah, that is just the problem.

ART, ETHIC, AND RELIGION 261

It cannot be taken for granted. It is a great problem both for religion and for philosophy, the great problem thought sets to faith, whether we may identify finality and causality, whether the Christ who is to crown all is the Christ who shapes all. Or rather, perhaps, we put it in the converse way — the Christ who is so mighty in history, has He the throne in eternity? We have marked in the history and nature of Art the action of certain processes of reconciliation, redemption, spiritualisation, and so on. How do we know that these will converge and close in a reconciliation and glorification of all things? Have we any access already in history to an act which is the final reconciliation and manifestation of the whole creation revealed in advance? Shall we rise and shine in the Light that is long already come? Are we already presented with the grand consummation? Does the Absolute emerge at an historic point? Has the Eternal Glory already lived among us and become a perpetual present and a constant power? Is there something already in historic experience for which all things work together? Now are we sons of God; will there be a conclusive manifestation of the sons of God and their eternal vindication? If we put it in æsthetic terms we ask: Allowing that an ideal beauty is at the core of things, are all things certainly working that out at last? The world is full of love and its beauty. Are all things working together for good to love, for love's consummation? Will it come to the top at last? Is that which is Nature's noblest instinct also secured as its supreme goal ? Are my own best instincts certain to work out to my best self, or to such a world as I dream might be ? Is artistic creation to be completed in its own way, and all Art to come to itself in the goal of the Great Creator's work ? Is the beautiful to come out with holiness on the crown of all the world at last ? It often seems dubious enough. There is some malign, deflecting, debasing influence at work. There is an untowardness in life as regards the things of the soul, whether in beauty, goodness, or truth. There seems a conspiracy against the soul. Art, like other high things, has to fight for its existence ; and to mere observation the battle still sways. May not the evil and earthy side yet win ? Is there any power at work to secure that it shall not, and secure us in the certainty that it shall not ?

Now, to that question Art, with all its ideas, all its ideals, has no answer. All its insight cannot make it perfectly steadily sure that the beauty it now feels it will one day enjoy for ever. It cannot be sure that the idea labouring in the world is the goal awaiting the world, that the world's principle is the world's destiny. That is a conviction that can only be given by Revelation and its answer, Religion, by faith, by the Christian faith of Redemption, and not by the artist's dream. All things work for final good, not to lovers of beauty, or of love, but of a saving God. That God is the reality of all, with the reversion of all. The key of creation is its redemption. It can come to itself only by being redeemed. For the æsthetic mind, indeed, it might be enough to believe in evolution, if we could be sure it would go on and meet no stronger degenerative power. But for the ethical mind that knows the moral world, evolution gives no sure footing. And conscience demands redemption in an act of faith. Precisely how faith gives this certainty I cannot stop to inquire here. It is the result of personal trust in an Eternal Person victorious in an eternal act. I only point out that it is faith's gift, and not art's. It is the first concern of faith to secure us in such a way that we shall be settled on this final and universal certainty. But such is not the business of Art. It can do much to deepen our sense of the spiritual *in* the world, and to strengthen a presumption that the spiritual may close the world ; but we have no right to ask Art to take the place of Religion, and assure us that the world must and shall close so. Art is not there to give us the *certainty* of faith in such a matter. Art is ethical in principle, but it is not ethical in function. It is not an ethical inspiration in the sense that the prophet is. It conveys, but it does not convince. It has an ethical foundation, but it is not there to give ethical security. A drama, an epic, a novel, a picture, a statue can set before us a new world within the world, and plant it in us in a most memorable way, a most exalted, refreshing way. It can reflect and represent life, its problem, its drift; its interior, its aspirations, and its great ventures, but it cannot give us assurance of God and His eternal venture among men. Art, for instance, can give us a portrait of the man as we never saw him, but as he deeply and truly is. It can set forth the confusions, the conflicts, the struggles of the soul, or the age, in a way so penetrating as to arrest and solemnise us, or so harmonious that we feel a certain noble satisfaction and grand surmise in the sight. *Hamlet* closes in blood, but amid floating hints and echoes of a vaster world that may enfold and straighten all. And in doing all this in a worthy way, Art is religious in the great sense. But, all the same, Art is not positive religion. It has not the same work as positive religion to do. Their ideas, their purpose, are different. The Art idea is universal *harmony* : which need not be a moral idea, but only an intellectual—a great σύνθεσις. But the religious idea is universal *reconciliation* (or redemption)— a great σύγχυσις; and if that is not moral, it is nothing, it does not reach the bottom of life. Religion and Art have each a moral effect. But in the one case it is direct, like a sermon, in the other it is indirect, like a poem. The artist's business is to present the problem in a way so noble that the form of the question is half the answer. But the other and weightier half is the prophet's business. It is the work of faith, and not imagination.

Art, indeed, is deliverance, and so is Religion. Each means a redemption. But one is by the æsthetic way, the other is by the moral. The one releases the mood, the other the personality. The one relieves the world's constriction of the

ART, ETHIC, AND RELIGION 265

aching heart, the other breaks the world's dominion over the guilty soul. The one refreshes, the other regenerates. The one can take the prisoned soul and lap it in Elysium; but Elysium itself is a prison to the soul touched with hunger and thirst for the living God; and it needs more than Art to make us freemen of the communion of God. Art delivers us, for the time at least, from the clashes and contradictions of life. We do not simply forget them; for Art is surely much more than an opiate. They seem, as in music especially, to be fused and harmonised before us, and we into the paradise thus made. We are lifted and placed where they melt into each other in a life within life. Our desires are transfigured or stilled. It is a warm bath for the soul in a sunny river of life, cleansing, cooling, soothing, restoring. We know not only peace, but elation. We come to rest in a heavenly fulness. But calm is not all, though calm is well. Joy is not all. It is not the victory that overcometh the world for good and all. The refreshment is not regeneration; we are not set to grow for ever by the river of life; it is release only, it is not redemption. The blessed hour does not endure. It is visitation, not possession, by the spirit. It is not life that is delivered, it is only experience. Earth resumes her reign. The hour passes; it throbs down with a dying fall; and we return to the old crises and distractions. It is transfiguration, it is not resurrection. But in Religion, on the other hand, the deliverance is a life matter, an eternal crisis. It affects the soul itself, and not simply its experience. It does not harmonise us within till it has reconciled us to One without. It is not rational even, as if its object were free thought; its object is the free soul. And its manner is not æsthetic, but moral. It lives on the act and miracle of the Divine Incarnation, and not the order and process of the divine immanence. For it comes by the great moral act of history and the universe—by Christ's death and Resurrection, and our communion of these. Art's deliverance is but the promise, or *aura*, of this Redemption, in which alone we are free for life and death, for good and all. There the wicked cease, not only from troubling, but from wickedness. We lose not only care, but death. And our world is not only harmonised, but it is atoned and redeemed and reconciled for ever. And this peace and power is not but whispered in the ear, it is seated in the soul. And its musicians know.

III

This difference between the idea in Art and the ideal in Religion leads to the suggestion of one reason at least for the suspicion and aloofness which have existed between Religion and Art. It is no use denying that in the New Testament Art and the beautiful hold a very secondary place—as far at least as the practice of the New Testament goes, whatever we may say of the principle of the Gospel. No doubt our Lord had a feeling for Nature, and a sense of its beauty. And we are told to pursue whatsoever things are lovely in conduct. But

ART, ETHIC, AND RELIGION

these facts, and others similar, often adduced, do not settle the case. The Church also, in most of its great phases, has been more alive, on the whole, to the perils of Art than to its charm, just as Jesus felt the perils of wealth more than its possibilities. And one explanation is, as I have said, that Religion has, above all things, to do with final reality, while Art is first concerned with the beautiful appearance of things, the gleam and pageantry of things. The greater and more ethical our faith is, the more it forces us upon reality. The certainty it gives us is that holy love is the deepest and last reality now and for ever. But Art not only does not give us this foundation for life; it is in very many of its forms careless of it, and in some against it. It can make men too delighted with the present to trouble about the Eternal, and too full of the transfigured appearance to a few to be interested in the glorious reality for all. It can even cast its glamour about evil, and make sin doubly engaging. It is not till a religion is in a very strong position that it can afford (for the sake of sinful men's fickle, inflammable, and presumptuous souls) to hold close terms with Art. For a long time the surface realism of Art makes more powerful appeal than the deep reality of Religion; and a cultured and sensitive society may be, and has been, inwardly hollow, cruel, and false. The solution of life's contradictions which we find in Art is, like all temperamental solutions, more delightful, and costs less, than that which comes by the Cross. And delight is so near, and God is so far. Art has its very nature in the materialising of the spiritual, in making sensible the supersensible; and it is so fatally easy to make the material and sensual the reigning tone. While the movement in Religion or conscience is the other way; it is to spiritualise the material. Many religions make God become a man, only one makes a man become God. To human nature it is much more easy to follow the one than the other; and the speech of sense to the spirit is so much more quickly understood than the word of the spirit to sense.

It is Christianity alone that does justice to both movements in the full faith of the Incarnation, the movement from heaven to earth and the movement from earth to heaven [1]—not as an interesting doctrine, but as an effective and creative principle.

IV

The artist has a moral difficulty all his own. 'Love not the world,' we are urged, ' nor the things of the world.' But if the artist do not love the world, and the things and shows in it, he can do nothing to the purpose. The man who pursues the world in the way of business may dislike, or somewhat despise, the people he has to deal with and the situations he has to handle. The city may be to him hateful, and he will get out of it as soon as he extorts from it the means. But his labour prospers, his battle is won, he achieves success, and attracts

---

[1] May I refer to the last chapter of my book *The Person and the Place of Jesus Christ*. Independent Press, 1946

ART, ETHIC, AND RELIGION

even the envy of those he despises. He can use the world for his purpose without loving it, and he can prosper without real affection for his calling, though not without earnestness in it. But the artist cannot do this. Even the religious man may reach spiritual success through comparative indifference to the world, and neglect of much that is meant by the natural man. He may become a great spiritual power without much in the way of human or cosmic sympathy. It is a youthful mistake to measure spiritual power by genial sympathy. The great saint or prophet may be somewhat cold or hard or harsh to his world. But the artist cannot. He must love that world of show that he handles. He must love the show of it. He must dwell on it because he loves it. He must pore on it till he loves it. Even if it is not the show merely that he paints, but the thing behind it, the idea, the spirit of Nature, whatever you call it, yet, unless he love this material and corporeal show, it will not yield its secret. The chemist wins from Nature *his* secret with only vigilance and patience, but the artist cannot elicit his except as a lover. The chemist questions, but the artist woos.

And surely it is a great thing for the heart that it should be bestowed on anything so vast, so fair, so endless, exquisite, and glorious as Creation is. What a liberal education it has been and is to many a soul. How we have suffered, how Religion has suffered, for want of that kind of culture to-day—from lack of an imagination educated by the love of real beauty, greatness, and majesty, as Nature offers them, or man.

But what a peril it is! That a soul with a rare power to love should have it for his vocation of genius to love the material, that a soul eternal should be specially equipped to bestow his passion upon a world of sense which is as fugitive as the tints of a sunset; that he can hope to do nothing in his art unless he thus love mightily something which has no moral quality, which cannot love him back, or, if it love, loves not in a moral way, but in a romantic or even a sensual way; that the artist's marriage with Nature should be a romantic marriage only, and not an ethical one, with the conscience all on his side and the beauty all on hers; that the bond should be but in the feeling of the present without the fixity of a sure promise; that it should be at the mercy of the feeling, and not secured by conscience; that his mood should become his law, and his genius his charter for anything; and that this bride should be but the creature of sense that Nature is to all except the triumphant geniuses who can force their way to her deep, reluctant soul, as Parsifal did to Kundry —all this makes for the artist a moral peril which no other profession shares (except, perhaps, the preacher who sinks to loving Christ for the sake of men more than men for the sake of Christ). What wonder, if for one to whom Nature is a wife and a home, there are many to whom she is a harem. What wonder if for one whose works are his honest children, there are many who leave but bastards and not sons. Or, on the other hand, what wonder that form should often be divorced from foundation, that the divine inseparables of soul and sense should be parted, that execution should take the place of inspiration, that development should become decadence, that Art should come not to care what it says if it say it well, and so sinks to the trivial, the banal, or the beast; that it should drop from revelation to titillation; that Art for Art's sake should descend to mean only Art for the artist's sake, and the Church of the beautiful be sacrificed to its priests; that the painter should forget in his genius that he is a man, and so lose his own soul.

It is required that a man be faithful to his vocation; but it is never required that he sacrifice his conscience to it. To do that is to sacrifice his manhood to his genius or to his profession, which is incompatible with an ethical religion, and certainly with the faith of Christ. To live to faith is to live to conscience and moral manhood. It is to these that Christ makes His appeal. It is to these He brings His help. And He helps these directly. Whatever He does for a man's genius is done through the conscience, which is so much more than genius. A man *has* a vocation, but he *is* a soul. In Christ alone soul and vocation were perfectly one. And it is by his soul's quality, *i.e.* by his religion, that a man must fulfil his truest vocation to Art. All must have a conscience, but all need not pursue Art or foster it. Art is not life —it enlarges and enriches life in a spiritual way, but it is not life. But faith is life—' a man's faith is his all,' says Luther—it is a need for all, and for artists as much as any, and more than many.

V

The artist is in more danger than most from a noble form of idolatry, the worship of the beautiful creature. He must worship and love. His relation to Nature is, if not wholly yet largely, temperamental. He cannot be as indifferent as many are to the world he handles. As a painter he is more than the world he paints, or its ideas. Christ is our supreme authority on spiritual values, and nothing in Christ's view is comparable with the soul. So if the artist love and worship Nature, he is in danger of spending himself on what is below himself. That is, he becomes unreal. And how, then, is his art to escape becoming unreal also at last?

The real world is not what Nature gives, but what conscience gives. A man is a real man, not as he lives with Nature, but as he lives with his conscience, lives centrally with his conscience (I do not mean at every hour, which might easily come to mean priggery). But in Nature there is no conscience. A living conscience, therefore, worshipping Nature confronts something lower than himself in dignity and reality. He loves and pursues with energy something without moral urgency or even ideal. If he spend himself wholly on this he is losing his soul, in the ethical sense of the phrase. He may be full of soul, as the saying is, but he is

ART, ETHIC, AND RELIGION 273

bestowing his moral self upon something not moral, or not yet moral; and surely that is throwing his soul's reality away. How much of the unreality in Art arises from this source! The artist loses the sense of the real by his error in bestowing his whole moral self on something morally unreal. The conscience which makes a true man craves always to find a like conscience behind what he loves most. And if he do not find it, he never comes fully to himself. He loses himself, though he gain the whole world of beauty. Art, in him or his school, becomes perfect and soulless, finished and inadequate, entirely correct and very unreal. Many an artist must say to himself, ' I have been painting but pictures, and I feel I was made for realities.' When a man feels like that, it is a confession that the reality of his own soul has as yet missed the great reality outside him and awaiting him. How shall he find it? Where does the moral soul and self find the moral reality for which it craves? Where can it find it but in God, and God's supreme, eternal, moral action? A person can only rest in a person, a soul in a soul. Nature and soul are alike unreal till they are settled on that rock. And that rock is practically Christ, for experience it is Christ. The moral God, the real God, the sure God, the Eternal God is with us only in Christ—the Christ of my experience and of man's. The certainty of God, the reality of Him, the love in Him, the holy beauty in Him, communion with Him, are ours only in the person of Christ. It is not at last a case of either touching God or being touched by

Him, but of living and habitual communion with Him, not of His presence, but His fellowship. For a soul to love the beauty and glory of Nature, and yet to find nothing to love, trust, and enjoy for ever behind it, is surely a fatal idolatry. It leaves the imagination with an object of passion, but not the conscience. Yet the passion of conscience is the greatest we can feel. And even Nature deserves the artist's greatest. She is so great that we cannot continue to do her justice if we are incapable of the greatest passion. We must worship a moral power above and within her. Speaking less of individuals, than of schools or tendencies, we are not fair or adequate to great Nature herself if we come to her witless of the moral passion behind her which sets man above her; if we do not realise that morality is the nature of things. Art dies if it be severed from this moral passion in any community. And the centre, source, and supreme object of moral passion is Christ; whom we love, not simply because of His moral beauty, but because of His moral victory for us, for our forgiveness, and the release of the world's conscience from guilt and doom.

VI

The peril I have named is aggravated by two other peculiarities. The artist in his work lives a self-sufficing life. His work is a joy and an end in itself. He is thus cast into sympathy chiefly with other artists. Not only is he tempted to take his feeling for his all, his impulse for his charter, and his genius for his justification, but he is in danger of regarding no public opinion but that of comrades with the same insulated habit of mind. He lives for an artist world, which may sink to a coterie. He too easily falls a victim to a morality merely professional, to the clericalism of his kind. He is tempted to despise the ethic of the Philistines, or only to exploit it in his patrons and buyers. His business is to experience a feeling quite different from other men in presence of the same things; and he is apt to fall into a class which is apart in its principles as well as its perceptions. He is tempted to divide mankind into two orders, artists and not artists, the choice and the common, the Brahmans of taste and the Pariahs of humdrum, the æsthetic mandarins and the ethic mob, the freemen of impulse and the slaves of convention, those to whom much is given and those of whom nothing can be expected, the peerage of genius and the plebs of duty. He comes to believe, as a Frenchman of the kind said, that 'Society to its roots is but a tissue of sickening humbug.' 'The crowd is always hateful!' This aristocracy of taste has no idea how great its ignorance is, nor how coarse its heartlessness. It loses the power of appreciating the greatness of its contemporaries, of owning the value of Society, of expressing the nation it belongs to, or of understanding the intellectual movements that make and mark the age. It becomes more shoppy than the shopkeepers it disdains, and more narrow than the bourgeoisie. And it loses both the sympathy and the control which the healthy and wise man finds in the social order and the public heart. There can be noted sometimes, alongside of the most cultured taste, an ethical anæsthesia which takes a gross form in such a character as Benvenuto Cellini, and an engaging form in ages of more general refinement and decency like our own. I cannot but think it betrays some moral obtuseness, some lack of moral self-knowledge, when there is placed on the grave of a fine and popular artist the words :

> A little hope that when we die
> We reap our sowing, and so good-bye.[1]

The retrospect gives him but a little hope, and he knows himself so poorly that he can find what hope he has in thinking he may be treated with strict justice, and will reap as he has sown. ' God, be merciful to me a sinner ' goes down to his narrow house far more justified than that.

Society cannot flourish upon a morality of taste —the ethic of the agreeable—as so much of the morality of current society is. It is ethically donnish at best, and selfish at worst. It may have a pleasant modesty, but not humility. It is set upon self-realisation, and all the punishment it undergoes is no more than any other phase of culture which goes to complete the pyramid of its own existence. No humiliation brings real humility (cp. Oscar Wilde's *De Profundis*). It is all but the exploitation of a fresh experience for the self-perfecting with which he is engrossed. Affliction is just another region of culture, and moral

[1] On grave of George du Maurier, Hampstead.

ART, ETHIC, AND RELIGION

discipline is but the culture of another taste in the pursuit of symmetry of character. 'I lived on honeycomb. I had to pass on. The other half of the garden had its secrets for me also. To have continued the same life would have been wrong *because it would have been limiting.*' The one thing he hopes not to feel is shame and its narrowing effect.

Now, it is true that a man's taste will sometimes be more modest and pure than his heart. His impulse may debase him where his taste protests and revolts. But the weakness of the position is that taste can do so little beyond revolting in the majority of cases. It cannot cope with impulse in the matter of force. Taste has not the power the heart has. Human nature can be moulded by good taste, but never mastered. It can be regulated, but not captured, and it can become decorous, but not loyal. Good taste is better than a bad coarse heart, but a good heart is better than good taste, and more effectual. The morality of taste grows thin, powerless, and hollow, a thing of good form, without depth, feeling, or sincerity. It prizes fine feeling more than deep or true feeling. It is the slave of charm and the foe of power. It debases the artist because it has no welcome for the prophet. It is all very well so long as inclination and duty coincide; but when they do not, taste either sophisticates us or is silenced. If there be any meaning in the phrase ' nonconformist conscience,' it is this—it is the assertion of moral power against moral taste.

There is a special action of morality in Art, but there is no special morality for the artist. He must live by the same general conscience as guides all mankind. Conduct is for him, if it is for others, three parts of life. In becoming artists we do not cease to be men. When we are out of immediate relation to Art, as in family, public, or Church life, we are still men. And after the artistic power is spent, it is as men, and not as artists, that we must die. Our art only interprets the Humanity we share; and the soul of this Humanity, which we must truly share to faithfully interpret, is a mortal, moral soul. It is by the conscience that we stand or fall before eternal and holy things.

Æsthetic refinement gives no dispensation from the obligations of the general and human conscience. Taste is not the moral standard. There are people who, if they are generous, think they need not trouble to be just; and in extravagant geniality they lose the pecuniary conscience. And there are men who will shrink from no cruelty or inhumanity for a mere sense of fantastic honour; and they will not only take a life but desolate a whole family in a duel. So also there are those who forgive a lie, but not an indelicacy, who care for honour, but not right, who live easily in an atmosphere of hypocrisy so long as it is good form, and who think that vice is not vice so long as it loses its grossness. But the mere refinement of an impulse does not give it a claim to rule the conscience, or to be a conscience. Delicate inclination is not duty. A generous passion can lead to the surrender of virtue.

ART, ETHIC, AND RELIGION

The sentimental moralist speaks in this wise: 'What are moral scruples in the face of my magnanimity, of my friends' suffering? May I not sacrifice my virtue to save my friend? Am I not really thinking egoistically of myself and my punishment when I plead my conscience against some impulse that seems noble and fine? What is bourgeois character that it should impede divine art, or what is the morality of Brown, Jones, and Robinson that it should interfere with the pursuit of high, new knowledge?'

To all which Goethe himself has the answer:

> Youth, remember! In the throbbing,
> In the flush, of sense and soul,
> That the muse is but a comrade,
> And her place is not control.

Art is not life, but an interpretation of life. And as an interpreter she is not life's guide, but life's distinguished friend. The guide of life speaks to life's conscience. And none can speak the last word to life's conscience but He who takes away its sin. The root of morality is not the art which appeals to some, but the Redemption which embraces all.

VII

The second peculiarity which adds to the artist's peril is this. When the common man yields to impulse, he yields to the overmastering violence of it. He does not try to persuade himself he has done right to yield. He treats his impulse as overwhelming him, but not as *entitled* to rule him.

So when the fit is over he knows and owns he has done wrong. He admits the claim and right of the law. He can repent and confess. There is hope for him. But the man of culture is apt to be too refined and subtle for this. He will deny that he has done wrong. Or if he takes his punishment, he can begin with a clean bill. 'If one is ashamed of having been punished one might just as well never have been punished at all,' said Oscar Wilde with a moral levity and dulness intractable to an awful judgment. He sophisticates himself. And by his wits and tastes he tampers with the moral standard. He tries to prove to himself and others that he had a certain right to give way. Either he declares that the law for the mass of people is not a law for elect geniuses; he claims that what is forbidden to Nature's serfs is allowed to Nature's lovers; he perverts Augustine and says, 'Love, and do as you will.' Or else he tries to make the law carry a refined meaning which justifies the sin by removing the prohibition. His subtlety, his sensibility, gives him a fatal acuteness in explaining away the conscience in the interest of his own pleasure, freedom, and symmetrical development.

But no man does justice to beauty till he feel the moral beauty of resisting beauty—upon due occasion. There is something incomplete in artistic taste until it see, with so great an artist as Plato, the beauty of Puritanism. This is a form of beauty that borders on the sublime, or passes into it. But the appreciation of it is hard and rare at the present

ART, ETHIC, AND RELIGION

day, when the sense of the sublime has been overwhelmed by the amateur's taste for the pretty, by the literary habit of pose, or by the newspaper taste for the big. The artist is in more danger than some other professions of losing taste for the moral heroisms which transcend Art or Sentiment. Yet, if the artist discard such things, Art does not; and it can find scope for its genius even in appreciating them, disinterring from their commonplace their moral value, and blessing them as they curse it. I am afraid the artist is sometimes more interested in those who are below Art through vulgarity than in those who are beyond Art through moral greatness, grandeur. And he calls his taste realism. There is not much beauty in mere insensibility to beauty, but there may be very much in its renunciation. There may be more beauty, more matter for Art, more reverence for Art, in the clergyman who refuses to touch his violin for years, because he was becoming its victim, than in those groups of art students, dear to Mürger and the Vie Bohème, who make a taste for Art the cover for vice and the minister of lubricity, who waste in gay idleness youth's most plastic time, and sow the seeds of all slackness, physical, mental, and moral. It is beautiful enough for artistic treatment to see all Art sacrificed *upon sound grounds* to the supreme and hardest art of living. And the true artist should be capable of answering to such a heroic pursuit of the ideal. He is *borné* if he feel no charm in an act like that, if he see there no theme for some form of art.

VIII

It would be ungracious to dwell on Art's moral perils. It has moral principles of its own, and a moral mission, however indirect. It is sometimes asked, Does Art exist for the artist chiefly or for the public—meaning by the public, of course, the sympathetic public? And it is often answered with some impatience of the artistic laity, that it is there for the clergy of Art, for the artist or for the virtuoso. This is a tendency which is not confined to Art, but extends to religion and many other interests. With the growing specialisation of life the position claimed for the expert becomes more and more exacting. And in the interest of Humanity and of the soul the claim must often be refused. The clergy is not the Church. Mere professionalism debases any profession. And an art that existed for the artists alone, or in chief, would soon suffer, and come to a poverty of sympathies and a bankruptcy of ideas. But there is a point of view from which it can be said that in a special sense Art is for the artists.

I mean more than the artist's natural and laudable desire for praise from his peers. I mean this. There must always be a great moral difference between those who are active in Art and those who are passive. We find it so in the inferior forms of recreation. The moral effect of sport upon the crowds who are merely spectators is very different from its action upon those who provide the spectacle. The most debasing effect of any kind

ART, ETHIC, AND RELIGION 283

of sport is that which it has upon the lazy mass of habitual onlookers. The players have the immense moral advantage of putting their energy into it. Their will is concerned. They are not only active, but they undergo a discipline of their activity. They submit to training. They endure hardship. They learn to act together, to emulate, to command their temper, and to keep the body under. The spectators, on the other hand, are in pursuit only of their own pleasure or excitement. They are plutocrats to the extent of the gate-money, and they enjoy only what money can buy. They are selfish, and they have no corporate feeling. They are a crowd and not a body. The masses of people who attend football matches or races are the real seat of the mischief that sport does. Now, *mutatis mutandis*, the same is true of Art, where the higher faculties play. The crowds that pass through the rooms of the Academy regard the artist much as the football crowds regard the players. The audience at a concert, too, is passive. It habitually surrenders itself to mere recipiency. The judgment is mostly lulled; for criticism is apt to kill enjoyment, and if it come at all, it comes after. The art public consents to the illusion which is so great and fine an element in Art. It agrees to make its judgment blind. It likes or dislikes without asking why. Its will is in abeyance. It abandons itself to a pleasure which it pays for by little or no effort. There is, therefore, no corrective to the moral perils of mere passivity, mere recipiency. And if they had nothing in life to do but surrender themselves from time to time to such pleasure, however elevated, the result could only be moral degeneration—as in many artistic communities it has been. And the artist also, unless he has some other standard than the taste of habitual dilettantists, is sure to suffer. But he has always a safeguard in the fact that it is his profession. He has to work at it. He has to put his will into his achievement. He has to go through a continual training. And he has to discipline his life accordingly.

Besides, if there were nothing else, there is this. Art calls for selection and choice. The true artist does not take the first thing that offers, and proceed to imitate it in paint. He is not the victim of the first experience he meets, nor the second, nor the third. From the many experiences of his mind he seizes on one or other group in particular. Why he is so arrested, he could not always say himself. There is the region where the mysterious breath of inspiration plays. But being arrested by his object he is detained on it. He detains himself, he selects ; he concentrates on it out of all the stream of experiences that flow in on him from a flashy, fleeting world. This concentration is an act of will and of judgment. It is a moral act and often a sustained act. It grows as it goes. It becomes prolonged and assiduous toil. He wrestles with a task. He compels himself to the conflict. He learns to dread the dabbler's habit of working only when the fit is on him. He will always lay the tinder so that he may never lose the spark. It is moral effort. It is will and conscience. The

ART, ETHIC, AND RELIGION

real difference between the artist and the dilettantist is just this of toil.

> The crime I ascribe to each frustrate ghost
> Is the unlit lamp and the ungirt loin.[1]

It is a moral difference. And the artist's success is a moral victory. This art makes a man of him as well as an artist. He has an artistic conscience which it is part of his moral duty to cherish against his weaker self and his clamorous public.

IX

If the artist give way to popularity, he is simply accepting the standard of those who are more or less demoralised by being perpetual recipients, not to say paupers. He sacrifices everything to meet the demands of beneficiaries, of people who sacrifice nothing, who do not work for their enjoyment, but who live on those who do. His art becomes the victim of its laity, as surely as at the other extreme it becomes the victim of its clergy. In this sense, therefore, the artist must feel that his art exists in a special way for him. He has a stake in it which his public has not. His will, his manhood, is in it, as it is not with his public. He bends to it every other energy, and he broadens it by a wide general culture. His attitude to his art cannot be that of a mere recipient. He must spend himself on it. He loves it so much because he makes sacrifices for it. He may even have to wrestle with it. For this reason we have great artists warning their scholars to beware of giving

[1] Browning: The Statue and the Bust.

themselves up to artistic dreaming or extemporising. They must write, compose, take a serious subject, and compel it into artistic form. If they only extemporise, they become a mere audience of their own. They glide down a stream, they but yield to impressions, and to impressions from their own subjectivity which may but coddle their own egoism. They are artistic, but they are not artists. To be artists they must call their will into play. They must use a selective, creative judgment. They must be makers, and not dreamers. And they must have in view a standard the public has not. 'When you play,' said Schumann, 'do not trouble who is listening. Yet always play as if a master were listening.' It is great advice. And it is truest of all applied to the most difficult art of life.

The artist, like the preacher, must beware of the public. His art is in peril if he live on its favour just as much as if he despise it. Popularity is a stimulant, not a food. It is the lowest art (if it be art at all) which is mere display, self-exhibition, posturing. If a man is in earnest at all his public will ruin him if it can, and if he allow it. They only want interest or amusement where he spends his soul. What for him is creation is for them but recreation. What for him is art for them is sport, just as the burden and passion and judgment of a gifted prophet may be treated by the flocking public as mere entertainment (cp. Ezek. xxxiii. 30). His works are their play. And there is always moral danger in putting one's soul into what is but

ART, ETHIC, AND RELIGION 287

amusement. I do not for a moment say that a public amuser follows an immoral vocation, but it is non-moral, and as a life-work it seems hardly in itself to contribute to ethical growth and spiritual dignity, unless special moral precautions are taken, or special spiritual grace sought. Art is for something else than to fill and please the passing moment. That is but sport or play; which produces nothing. But art is a producer. It leaves real works behind it, and it handles eternity in some fashion. It has the instinct of the immortal and the Spirit of the Eternal. There is something which outlives the delight of each exhibition or performance, and is exhaustless for many such. The thing most valuable for the artist is the hidden labour, the moral victory, the spiritual conquest and satisfaction which are involved in the mastery first of his ideas, then of his technique. But this is not what the public cares for, though it is what tells on Humanity at last.

The artist then becomes a master of his art quite as much by certain moral qualities as by his technical or his æsthetic. And the spring of moral strength and staying power is Religion. If that be not so for every individual, it is so for history and for the race. And if Religion be taken in earnest, in as much earnest as a genius takes his art, it must be something else than pantheistic religiosity, which discourages personality and moral effort. It must be the personal religion of Jesus Christ. It must be personal faith in Him. We may sit very loose to many views once called essential. We may even be somewhat indifferent to a church. And we may be free in our treatment of the Bible. But the personal rule over us of Christ, our personal committal of our soul to Him with all its powers, and our personal communion with Him, is the condition of a moral manhood as fine as genius or taste. It will be the crown of genius in the social future. To save a man from the public and make him a blessing to the public, that problem of genius in a democracy—for this the secret is still with Christ above all other influences that act on men. But in so saying, it should be clear that the Christ merely historic and humane is not equal to the perennial control of an interest so great and unusual as Art's treatment of Nature's text. It is a power that can be exercised by a dogmatic, universal and final Christ only, whether we accept the precise form of the dogma from the past or reconstruct it to our more modern thought and experience. Nothing less than a dogmatic Christ is adequate to the spiritual control of the greatest aspects and interests of mankind in every age.

X

If a man really believe in God through Jesus Christ, and have made to Christ the final self-committal, his art is not the *only* thing into which he will put his faith. He will put it also into the use to which he turns his art. If art were religion, then the artist could only be a purist. His principles of conduct would be loftily æsthetic. He would develop a fastidiousness which would

ART, ETHIC, AND RELIGION

unfit him for many of the duties of life. For the tendency of art alone, art as a religion, is to hallow life by retiring from it rather than sharing it. He would feel he was debasing his art if he pursued any but the highest reaches of it. If he came to earn an income from it he might be uneasy. If he married he might feel his genius was stunted, as Romney did. If he used it to support his wife and family he might feel it was sacrilege. If he produced correct and beautiful drawings for any of the advertising, decorative, or mechanical purposes of life he might feel it was profanity. These are examples of the extravagant purism of the devotees of art for art's sake, to whom art is their only religion. Need I point out how it narrows life, how it stunts the soul, how it breeds a Byzantine and monkish type of life, and a kind of morality either timid and cloistered, or hectic and defiant? If art were encouraged to prescribe morals, it would be set to do what it was never meant to do, and does badly. But religion does prescribe them. Morals must root in religion. So that if art were religion, art ideals would be our only morality. But if art be not religion, then we must seek the religion, even of art itself, elsewhere. If we are to have guidance for art, faith in Christ must give it at last. A church cannot. And it cannot guide itself. It cannot be its own religion. It cannot take the place of religion. Fantasy is one thing, and faith is another; and it is faith that guides life; and it guides art as a part of life. But it guides much besides. It guides the use we put art to. And it justifies, and even dignifies, us in using our art (so long as it is good art of its kind) for the purposes of a living, or to meet healthy public need. We may not use it for vice, and we may not use it to meet every public demand. But even placard art need not be vulgar. We are not obliged to confine art only to classic productions, or high art alone. Purity is not purism. We may serve public need, and our own honest necessities, so long as we do not allow our drudgery to smother our aspiration, our honesty, and our love of finer things. And is there anything which keeps aspiration, sympathy, and even taste, so clear of the drudgery entailed on us by some of life's offices and duties as the faith of Christ's salvation and the love and service of His moral beauty and ever-present perfection?

But I confess, if I were an artist and had to live by my pictures, I think I should find it a serious moral problem how to keep an Art conscience, and yet paint such pictures as the public to-day would buy. If Art is to be raised, it is the public that must be raised. And that Art cannot do. It is not an evangelist, or a prophet, or a moral reformer. It cannot start a moral regeneration in a people debased by money and uplifted by faith. It is a religious reformation that can alone do the thing that Art most needs to have done. The best service Religion could do Art would be to regenerate the public that counts with some worthy moral passion, deliver it from current moral vulgarity, and quicken it with some great spiritual enthusiasm.

ART, ETHIC, AND RELIGION 291

If Religion could only compel even its own public to take it more seriously! With popular religion so little of an ethical teacher, and public education so suspected as the average man suspects it, it is not the artists that are most to blame for the state of art. It is the public, and the religion offered to the public by many representative authorities of that religion in all the Churches. None are so interested in the revival and reform of Religion as the artists, if they would but cultivate as much mind as to measure the age and their deep spiritual implication in it.

The root of the triviality in so much contemporary art is in the public frame of mind, more even than in the artists themselves, when we go deep enough. The effect of an artist's personal religion on his own art work may be very indirect and small. Bad men have been consummate artists. And a saintly man might produce art of the most banal kind, just as he might have the practical judgment of a hen. But the effect of an age's religion, or a nation's, on art is always great. These large moral forces need more than the area of an individual life to range in and work out their results. They do not come home except on large planes and long periods. A great genius expresses much more than his own personality. He is the index, the hierophant, of an age, a people, the public soul. Turner's personal habits had no direct effect on his art. He did not utter his own soul, but a far larger something, which the vice of one lifetime could not reach. If this larger something be wrong or impious, it must tell on art and artist both. The artist may not paint better because he prays; but if prayer vanished art would certainly be materialised and trivialised in the general moral decay. An artist prays, when he does pray, not as an artist, but as a man. The effect on his art is the effect, not of his praying, but of the moral manhood that must pray. It is prayer that gives manhood its highest moral courage by teaching it not to be shy of the Almighty Power, but to trust it, love it, and converse with it. Of course if this moral manhood have no effect on art, there is an end of the matter. But if it have, on the whole, and on the larger scale, then it must make a good deal of difference whether art is plied by men of faith or not, whether the moral tone of artistic circles is one of faith or not, whether faith in anything spiritual be the note of the community. It may be long before it affect their execution, their craftsmanship; but it cannot be long before it affect their insight, their ideas, the spiritual quality of their art. And inasmuch as the artist is very sensitive to the form and pressure of his time, if he inhabit a faithless, and naturalistic, and mammonistic age he cannot but betray its influence, unless he is uplifted by a mightier power— were it only by his susceptibility to the oversoul or spirit of the world.

I do not say that to paint well a man must 'take an active interest in God' (as I have seen it strangely put). But if the public mind, especially in its higher forms, do not do what that odd phrase im-

ART, ETHIC, AND RELIGION 293

plies, if its *Weltanschauung* do not enthrone God, then Art, as one of the finest and most sensitive of human energies, must quickly feel and show what the public mind comes to without the moral courage of trusting God.

XI

Let us therefore not ask, ' How is religion to help my art ? ' That is æsthetic egoism. Let us ask, ' How is my art to help my religion ? ' And lest religion become egoist also, let us frame the question thus, How is Art to serve the Kingdom of God ? Man's chief end is not to be an artist, but to glorify God and enjoy Him. Art is not life, and faith is. Art does not prescribe a morality, and faith does. Christ did not come as a subject for Art, but as an object of faith and a giver of life. The artist needs Christ in the same sense as every other man, though not perhaps in the same form. The particular form of Christ's ministration to us varies with our vocation. It is in our vocation and not outside of it that we are to serve Him first of all. There is no pursuit in life in which we are not tempted to evade Christ. And art has its own form of doing without Him. It is difficult in business to keep a conscience. It is very hard to be a minister of the Gospel and ideally religious. It is not easy in the pursuit of science to keep the Christian humility. If the temptation of science is pride, and of religion is unreality, that of Art is sense or soullessness, luxury or triviality. It has its own form of self-sufficiency. It is apt to believe that Christ's

Gospel has nothing to do with culture, salvation with beauty, or moral stringency with æsthetic genius. You find men saying the same thing in politics, science, or business : that the best thing Religion can do is to get out of the way when the real conflict begins, or real business is to be done. That means, of course, that the religion of Christ belongs to our spare time, our less strenuous hours, our ornate sentiments; that it is sectional, that it does not deal with the whole man, that the engrossing passion of the man of genius is out of any relation to the same man's passionate faith. But that surely cannot be, if he have such a faith. There is a totality about men of real genius. And nothing that so engrosses a man's noblest part as Art does can be shut off water-tight from his worship. His imagination and his conscience cannot worship different gods without suppressing one faculty. We cannot serve God and Nature with equal devotion.

The only worshipping conscience is not the artist's, but the man's. There is, indeed, such a thing as the artistic conscience, but that is not the same thing as the artist's conscience. The key of the world in which we have to do our duty is not the artistic conscience, but the human. The moral world is the world of all of us, the æsthetic is the world of but a few. Every scheme of life or form of religion based on an æsthetic view of the world has broken down. The last reality is an ethical one. We come to that when all our æsthetic notions of life have failed us. The moral universe

ART, ETHIC, AND RELIGION

is not there for Art, but Art is there for the moral universe. And the heart of the moral universe is God; and its bane is sin; and the revelation and power of God is Jesus Christ on His Cross for its moral restoration.

The artist is not a great and fine Nature power, but an energy of the power that made Nature. Forgive me for repeating a valuable quotation. 'If an artist,' says Baader, 'paint a lion with genius, his success is not in merely copying the creature. But that creating nature which brought the lion forth meets the creature again in the imagination of the artist, and continues in the picture the work which began the beast.' The artist works by inspiration. Therefore he works for the Inspirer. And his art is there to serve his religion more than his religion to serve his art. We do not ask, therefore, what art will gain from faith, but how it can serve it, and be a piece of worship.

Of all producers the artist gives us the highest idea of God's creative work. There is nothing more analogous to God's production of men than Shakespeare's production of his characters and his world.

But we are fallen on an age of evolution and not creation, of execution and not inspiration, of mechanics not ideas, of organisation not origination. Therefore the originality of the artist and his way of working is under neglect. Is it easy for an age to believe heartily in God the Creator if it have little understanding of creative activity in men of genius?

But it is the man of genius himself who most feels how inadequate his creations are. He has but moments in which he rejoices in his work. In the conception there is joy, in the production there is labour and sorrow. He cannot get into line, colour, shadow, and tone the gleam, the glow, that he has in his imagination. 'Would that I could make it grow in my hands as it grew in my soul!' And so his skill toils after his inspiration in vain, and he can but prophesy in part what he sees as a whole. And here it is that the æsthetic experience concurs so deeply with the ethical experience. 'The good that I would I do not, but the evil that I would not, that I do.'

What is left us but to cast our pictures and our lives both upon the merciful and sympathetic construction of the perfect and faithful Creator, Who brings to bear on them an imagination more mighty and tender than man's, and Who can read out of our defects all our most splendid intentions, and out of our failures all we aspired to be, Who is our comfort in all we are not, and our Saviour from all we should not be. 'Life,' says one, 'is a perpetual second best.' Does the artist feel otherwise with art?

> Yet still a perfect God is He,
> And He is wholly ours.[1]

We are complete only in Him. In the great organic series it needs the workman to complete the work, and God to complete both. Only in Him do will and work entirely blend, and execution fully

[1] William Bright (1824-1901)

represent purpose. He is what we but toil to be. He is what His world but slowly and hardly becomes. We can never become what He means, but by faith in what He is, and what He has done to make us so. Faith is life's creative power. When we find our true place in His creation, we become creators also in our subordinate way. And we find our place by faith, and faith is the most creative power given to man.

THE END

www.ingramcontent.com/pod-product-compliance
Lightning Source LLC
Chambersburg PA
CBHW050337230426
43663CB00010B/1886